AF191954

# Alex Dreppec

# Tanze mit Raketenschuhen

# Dance with Rocket Shoes

## Wissenschaftsgedichte

## Science Slam Poetry

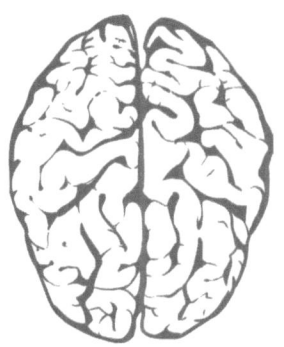

Im chiliverlag erschienen (Auswahl):

Glasaugenstern, 101 Gedichte von Alex Dreppec

Fassadenflucht, Politische Dichtung der Gegenwart II

suchtraum, Sandra Stubbe, Roman

Herzschlaf, Gedichte und Kurzprosa über Trauer, Trost und Hoffnung

Stimmwirbel – Gedichte, Michel Ackermann

Machen! Silben, Sätze, Sensationen, Marc Mandel

Gatti – Katz'n, 21 krasse Katz'nstories

Kodex Rosebud, Hans-Jörg Kühne, Roman

Kiss Me Cyprus Hell, Miriam Sonntag, Jugendroman

Abschreibungen, Lyrisches und Satirisches von Stefan Krückmann

Provozia, Ronald Zieger, Roman

Schwellenbrand, Helena Ende, Roman

wir wölfe – Gedichte, Eine poetische Hommage an unsere Tierwelt

Verstummung, Tier- und Naturschutzkrimis

Pappalappa Mirzapan, Gedichte für besondere Kinder

1. Auflage Dezember 2016

(c) chiliverlag, Franziska Röchter, Verl

franchili / 48

Die Rechte an den einzelnen Texten sowie Abbildungen liegen beim jeweiligen Autor.

Detaillierte bibliographische Daten sind unter http://dnb.ddb.de bei der Deutschen Nationalbibliographie abrufbar.

Gestaltung, Layout, Lektorat: chiliverlag

Cover nach einer Idee von Alex Dreppec

Übersetzungen: Alex Dreppec unter Mitwirkung (Lektorat) von Heather Rechel, Lawrence Nicholas, Chris Hughes, Harold Nash, Michael Reibold

Cartoon Seite 164: Axel Röthemeyer

Foto Seite 176 und auf dem Backcover: Ellen Eckhardt

Plakat Seite 180: André Liegl

Printed in Germany

ISBN 978-3-943292-50-3                    **www.chiliverlag.de**

Für meine Mutter / for my mother

Gabriella Deppert 1935 - 2016

# INHALT / CONTENT

## II Geist und Kunst / SPIRIT AND ARTS

8

## III Natur / NATURE

## IV Technik / ENGINEERING

# VORWORT DES AUTORS

Obwohl die vorliegenden Gedichte nicht dem – nicht-poetischen – Genre des Science Slam zuzuzählen sind, hat ihre Entstehung mit der des Science Slam zu tun: Als ich mit diesem als Organisator / Moderator anfing, begleitete mich stets die anfangs durchaus berechtigte Befürchtung, nicht genug Vortragende zu finden, um einen Abend zu füllen. Deshalb überlegte ich, was ich dem von Anfang an großen, an Wissenschaft interessierten Publikum noch bieten könnte und begann, Gedichte zu wissenschaftlichen Themen zu schreiben, um selbst das Rahmenprogramm anreichern zu können. Dies geschah nicht mit der Absicht, zu wissenschaftlichen Erkenntnissen beizutragen.

Im Lauf der zurückliegenden Jahre entstand die hier vorliegende Sammlung, die in großen Teilen vorher bereits abgedruckt wurde. Bei den englischsprachigen Texten werden hier gegebenenfalls die Zeitschriften und Anthologien angegeben, in denen sie vorab veröffentlicht wurden, da dies im englischen Sprachraum üblich ist und erbeten wird. Die Vorab-Veröffentlichungen im deutschen Sprachraum sind entsprechend nicht aufgelistet, obwohl sie weitaus zahlreicher sind (die große Mehrzahl der englischsprachigen Übersetzungen wurde erst relativ kurzfristig für diesen Band erstellt). Wer sich darüber informieren möchte, sei auf www. dreppec.de verwiesen.

Bei der Selbst-Übersetzung habe ich mir die Freiheit genommen, inhaltliche und/oder formale Änderungen vorzunehmen, wenn das dem Gesamtergebnis diente, bis hin zu der Entscheidung, einzelne Texte nicht zu übersetzen.

## PREFACE OF THE AUTHOR

Although the present poems cannot be counted among the – non-poetic – genre of science slam, their origin has to do with the latter: When I started organizing the science slam, I was always afraid not to find enough lecturers to fill an evening – for good reasons initially. So I thought about what else I could offer the big audience interested in science that attended the slams from the start. I began to write poems on scientific matters to be able to enrich the supporting program on my own. This was not done with the intention of contributing to the scientific gain of knowledge.

Over the past years, the present collection developed, large parts of which have already been published. Regarding the English poems, the magazines and anthologies in which some of them were printed previously are referenced as the original publisher here, as expected in the English speaking world. The first publications in German are not listed, though they are far more numerous (the vast majority of English translations has been created shortly before this publication). Those who wish to read up on the original German publications may do so on www.dreppec.de.

During the process of self-translation, I felt free to make substantial and / or formal changes when this was useful to the overall result, up to the decision not to translate individual texts at all.

## BOXENTON UND GEISTESBLITZ
(SCIENCE SLAM OPENER)

Seid keine Geiseln des Gefasels
von näselnden Schnöseln,
sondern befreit mit dem Flusensieb
Flausen von Phrasenbröseln.
Handreichungsfußnoten
abgeschüttelt in Stroh und Gras,
Weinbrand füllen die Boten
in Brennglas und Opernglas.
Aus allen Lexika wanken
wortgewaltig (Schrift)gelehrte.
Acht aufgescheuchte Gedanken
folgen ihrer Schriften Fährte.
Sie wollen mit versierten
Kapazitätenzitaten,
elegant elaborierten
Laborelaboraten
im Lichtschein stehen,
wo von Bühnenrändern
neue Ideen wehen,
und dann weiter schlendern.
So wird das Mikrophon
hier zum Geistessitz,
von dem auf bunten Wegen
Kabel Lunten legen
hin zu Boxenton
und zu Geistesblitz.

## SPEAKERS FOR SCINTILLATION
(SCIENCE SLAM OPENER)


Don't be held captive, be trapped
by nasal snob's big drivel crap,
free this pie in the sky, this lame gush
from phrases' crumbs with the (lint) brush.
Shaken off footnotes and handouts lie
around in the straw and down in the grass,
while on the stage, all the messengers fly
and fill brandy in spyglass and opera glass.
See scribes waver out of their encyclopedias,
they become bright and magniloquent.
Eight flushed thoughts will conquer all media,
bound to follow the track of their writing's scent.
They want to stand in the light with capacity's
quotations, they will fight opacity
where microphones borrow the spirit sound,
where ideas use stages to stroll around.
Speaker cables lay fuses to feed inspiration
from science to audience, to brain scintillation.

# BEI TUMBER PFLICHTLEKTÜRE

Wo selbst Milben verborgen ins Polsterbett husten,
wird Staub nicht mal weniger wenn man ihn schluckt.
Dieser wurde von Anfang an mit gedruckt.
Versuche nicht, ihn von den Seiten zu pusten.

Kurz davor gänzlich dein Sitzfleisch zu garen
und von sauren Gurken schon mehr als nur satt,
entlüftest du schließlich das Körperteil matt,
unter dem sich die Milben im Polster paaren.

Du kannst: das Buch toasten anstatt zu studieren
und weiterhin bleischwere Lettern zu kritzeln,
versuchen, am Innenohr selbst dich zu kitzeln
und dir mal mit Post-Its den Bart epilieren.

Statt in trostlosen Sälen matt unterzugehen
und dich mit Trübsal zu drangsalieren,
kannst du deinen mittleren Finger massieren
und mit ihm hoch erhoben im Freien stehen.

Beeile Dich lieber mit diesem Adieu,
denn wenn sich hier erst mal die Kreise schließen,
dann wird's aus geöffnetem Schließmuskel schießen,
bei „D", zwischen „Derrida" und „Diarrhoe".

# DURING STUPID REQUIRED READING

In the seat pads, hear some of the hidden mites sneeze.
Just don't try to blow all this dust off the pages,
cause it has been part of the printing for ages.
You swallow the dust, but it still won't decrease.

Before cooking your chair glue, oppressed is your backside,
overfed with the bilgy gooseberry sauce,
you deflate the part that's infected by dross,
under which takes place the mating of dust mites.

You can also, instead of just studying the book
and its grave leaden letters, simply first toast it,
or epilate your ragged beard with a post-it
and tickle yourself at the inner ear's nook.

Instead of perishing limply in gloomy halls
and harass yourself with affliction,
just give your left middle finger some friction,
rise it high, step outside of these goony walls.

Say goodbye soon, because that's the idea:
if once the dumb circles close all around here,
it will shoot out of open sphincters, I fear,
in section „D", between „Derrida" and „diarrhea".

17

# 1

# Sozial / Human

## WENN UNTERBEWUTZTES ZUM VORSCHWEIN KOMMT

### (für Psychologen)

Dein begrunztes Selbstbewutztsein
kommt nicht ohne Grunz zum Vorschwein.
So saut's nunmal aus hier, Thorsten
wenn sau alle Dämme borsten.
Schwart' und eberleg doch mal:
es ist auch für gruns ne Qual,
dass Dir immer Böses schweint
wenn man's Eisbein mit Dir meint,
wenn Du mit Schweinshaxenfaxen
nicht aufhörst auf gruns rumzuhacksen.
Schmalz ob Dir nach der Leber trachtet
wer Dein Eber-Ich nicht achtet.
Willst gruns Du in die Würste schicken,
den Spieß umdreh'n, den Nacken spicken?
Niemand hat doch je gewitzelt
weil Du am Kass'ler unbeschnitzelt
schweinheilig Dein Tagwerk werkelst
und durch Tal und Bergwerk ferkelst.
Schweiner Dich nicht in Ragout!
Ohne gruns wurst schweinsam Du.

# WHEN THE SUBGRUNTIOUS OINKS TO THE SURFACE
### (for psychologists)

Don't shoat your door unless off we go,
we respect your super-pigo.
Trough the wurst things overboard.
The sun will swine trough. Braise the lord.
Live and cutlet liver, you said.
Gammon, rehognize, it's sow bad:
From dusk till brawn, a boaring dirt ride.
You're sow pigged, bats in the belfried.
We spam on common ground pork, Sam,
the future's not Black Forest ham,
a farrow strip of land will do,
stop acting as in blind ragout.
Don't runt away from feelings, free them.
Don't ignore these chop signs, see them.
Stop bristle blowing. „Pork's not dead"? These
words sow us what's in your head cheese,
this dark wurst case scenario
tails you of pig mistakes, they show:
boned day you'll walk, without a coin,
the loin and windy roast aloin.

# AKZENTUIERUNG

(für Psychologen)

Frau Sieda war ängstlich denn sie
litt sehr unter Spinnenphobie.
Erst Gegenkonditionierung
verhalf zur Akzentuierung.
Nun süßt sie die Spinnen mit Süßli
und schneidet sie sich dann ins Müsli.

## ACCENTUATION
(for psychologists)


The fearful lady Miss Sobia
suffered from arachnophobia.
All kinds of help didn't change a thing
except of counterconditioning.
Now she sweetens the spiders with Nutrasweet,
chops them into her cornflakes to have some meat.

## MITEINANDER REDEN: 4
(für Psychologen, sowie mit besonderer Verehrung für
Friedemann Schulz von Thun)


Ich hatte mich wohl ausgiebig verlaufen.
Handyakku leer, kein Plan in Sicht.
Es gab auch nirgends mehr etwas zu kaufen.
Die Gegend wurde mäßig und dann schlicht.
Zum Schluss gar gänzlich weit entfernt von edel.
Ich hatte schon genug, das reichte aus.
Da hielt mir wer ne Knarre an den Schädel
und sprach: „Nun rück mal alle Kohle raus."

Das fand ich nun im Ton doch etwas rauer.
Der Mann war sichtlich keinesfalls geschult.
Ich wollte da was ändern, doch genauer:
Hab Schulungsschritte mit ihm abgespult.
Ich sprach: „Ich zeige Dir, wie ich es gut geschafft hab,
das, was hilfreich ist, ganz aufzunehmen.
Schick ne positive Ich-Botschaft ab.
Du brauchst Dich der Gefühle nicht zu schämen.

Ich weiß, dass Du verletzt bist und trotzdem:
Nun sage doch das Positive erst.
Dann lösen wir gemeinsam das Problem.
Es bringt ja nichts, wenn Du Dich nur beschwerst.
Der trock'ne Sachaspekt, der sicher darin steckte,
dass Du mir mit der Pistole drohst,
verdeckt beziehungsseitige Aspekte,
durch die Du ganz alleine nur verrohst.


b. w.

# FOUR SIDES OF COMMUNICATION
(for psychologists)


It seemed I had completely lost my way.
Where I was? I didn't have a clue.
The houses were pervaded by decay.
My cell phone battery was empty, too.
Not hard to guess, I felt a little bad.
I was about to ask him where to go
when that person held a gun right to my head
and said: „You squirt, now pass me all the dough."

I thought that was a little rough in tone.
This man wasn't yet trained, as you could see,
because of social patterns he had shown.
So I reeled training steps with him emphatically
to change that, and I said, „I'll show you how
to bridge the gap in such communications.
Just send a positive I-message now.
This will encourage your growth and maturation.

I don't want to force you onto the defensive,
I know you're hurt, I appreciate your values,
but for your feeling's balance it may be expensive
not to reflect on your pessimistic worldviews.
The dry and sober factual information
that's shown by how your gun's now pointing at me
obscures some aspects of the situation
like our relationship and how it's meant to be.

pto

Ja, klar, auf der Apellseite besteht noch
Dein Wunsch nach Bargeld, bestenfalls im Nu.
Aber die Selbstoffenbarung zeigt doch:
echte Arbeit traust Du Dir nicht zu.
Aufgrund von Du-Botschaft und Selbst-Etikettierung
ist „Taugenichts" wohl jetzt Dein Selbstkonzept.
Dass Du nicht echt wirkst, liegt an der Maskierung.
Das hat die Ich-Entwicklung wohl verschleppt.

Implizit bittest Du mich um Beistand
indem Du die Pistole auf mich hältst
als der, der sich nie von Problemen frei fand,
denen Du Dich ohne Austausch doch nicht stellst.
Das schließ ich induktiv, hör Dir ja aktiv zu,
geh diesen Schritt mit mir in eine bess're Zeit,
dann wird es konstruktiv, Du wirst ein andres Du
und Du fühlst Dich selbst am Ende ganz befreit."

Der Mann lachte erst irre, lief dann fort.
Ihn geh'n zu lassen fiel mir etwas schwer.
Durch Schulung wird die Welt ein bess'rer Ort.
Und so rief ich ihm denn auch noch hinterher:
„Du weißt. du kannst nicht nicht kommunizieren!
Auch eine Flucht sagt daher immer etwas aus!
Flieh vor dir selbst, dann wirst du dich dadurch verlieren
– hör zu, dann lernen wir gemeinsam draus.

Ich biete mich Dir an als Dein Berater,
auf dass Du Dich gestärkt im Alltag schlägst.
Ich erinner' Dich vielleicht an Deinen Vater
weil Du Emotionen überträgst.
Die Pistole da, die ist doch nur Fassade,
mit der Du selbstverschleiernd imponierst.
Zwischenmenschlich ist es einfach schade
wie Du Aggressionen projizierst."

Yes, of course, on the side of the appeal,
there's the desire you expressed here in a flash.
Self-revelation still does show us how you feel:
You don't trust yourself to really work for cash.
„Good for nothing" seems to be your self-concept.
To overcome this bad self-labeling's now the task.
Don't be ashamed of feelings, open and accept.
You're not authentic 'till you stop to wear that mask.

By holding this gun right here to my head,
you ask for help and we should really rearrange.
Constructiveness will solve problems instead.
I offer you an active interchange.
You'll get brutalized by feeling you're subprime.
My active listening posture's bound to help you, too.
Go this step with me into a better time
and in the end you'll find you'll be another you."

He laughed like crazy, then he ran away.
To let go of him for me was disagreeable.
There were so many things I had to say.
I cat-called at him what had become most seeable:
„You know you cannot not communicate!
Thus, your escape speaks in clearest terms to me.
Just turn around now, yet it's not too late!
This shows social competence, you'll see!

I remind you of your father, that is why
you do transmit emotions and they rise.
The gun is the façade with which you try
to bloat yourself in total self-disguise.
As your consultant, I will offer you a frame
to strengthen you in three talking sessions.
Cause interpersonally, it's just a shame
how you are projecting your aggressions."

## KOPF IM SCHREDDER

(für Sozialpädagogen)

Ungeöffnet stapeln sich in Ecken hier die Briefe,
bei Öffnung springen Rechnungen und Mahnungen
ans Licht.
Den Mann zieht es hinab als ob der Sarg schon
nach ihm riefe,
was ihm noch bleibt, erkennt er mit geschloss'nen
Augen nicht.

Hol ihm seine Hoffnung aus dem Ausguss, aus
dem Schredder,
das passt unter die Fußmatte, was der noch von sich hält,
hat sich in tausend Fallstricken verfangen und verheddert,
doch er hat nur diese Tage und er hat nur diese Welt.

# HEAD IN THE SHREDDER
### (for social pedagogues)


Unopened letters pile up in corners all around,
while opening these letters, unpaid invoices jump to light.
As if the coffin's calling after him, the man is pulled
                deep down,
with his eyes closed, what he still has is always
                out of sight.

Take his hope out of the shredder, his thoughts
                out of the drain,
his self-esteem's below the doormat, it is tramped down,
                furled.
He's been caught in many traps, so many snares
                inside his brain,
but he's only got these days and he has only got this world.

# UNTERFÜHRUNG

(für Sozialpädagogen)

Unterführung, Unterkunft urbaner Unglücksraben.
Umriss: Unikate unterlaufen, untergraben
unbegrenzte, uferlose Unannehmlichkeiten und
ungesunde Unterkunft und ungesunden Untergrund.

Unbequemen Unterständen, Unterwelten unterstehen
Unordnung, Unebenheit und ungeseh'nes Untergehen.
Unter unbeachteten, urbanen Umgehungen
unternehmen Unglücksraben unbeirrt Umdrehungen.

Unversehens unterhalten unbändige Unterkiefer
Unrat-Unterwanderungen, ungezählte Ungeziefer,
Ursuppen-Usurpator, unbelehrbar, unvergleichlich.
Unscharf: Uraufführung. Unterschätzung unausweichlich.

## UNDERPASS

(for social pedagogues)


Unbossomed unbelief, unheard until untold
underworld's underlings unzip, unpack, unfold.
Unnumbered undertones, unbarred unconsciousness,
underachievers, unfertilized unless
under umbrellas, uprising unknowingly,
underpass underdogs unfold unguardedly.

Untamed undertow, uncovered underground:
us, untangling uncharted ultrasound.
Unheard underdog's unwanted uprightness:
unconfirmed uproar, uncashed utterly unless
under umbrellas, uprising unknowingly,
underpass underdogs unfold unguardedly.

previously published in „Borderlands. Texas Poetry Review", 39, 2013

# DIE NACHHUT DER PASSANTEN

(für Sozialpädagogen)

Die Nachhut der Passanten zieht
hinter sich her die
Trümmer ihrer Häuser,
auf Rinnstein abonniert, swingt
zu Bipolar-Bebop,
am baumlosen Berg,
an Mauern entlang
im Schneckenüberschall.

Die Nachhut der Passanten, ver-
einzelt und verstreut von
vergangenen Kämpfen, sucht
vollen Unterhalt in
karger Unterhaltung, sucht ihr
Selbst in Selbstgesprächen: was wir in
alten Jahren waren und in
neuen Jahren wären.

Die Nachhut der Passanten liegt
unter einem Schirm mit abge-
knickten Rippen im Laternen-
schatten: ein entgrenzter Wohnort,
des Schirmherrn Domizil.
Da geht die Pappe, auf
der man liegt, schnell
auch als Dachpappe durch.

b. w.

## THE REARGUARD OF THE PASSERS-BY
(for social pedagogues)

The rearguard of the passers-by
pulls the debris
of its houses,
is subscribed to the gutter,
swings to bipolar bebop
on treeless mountains,
along walls at a
snail's supersonic speed.

The rearguard of the passers-by,
homeless and scattered by
the past's struggles, it seeks
full maintenance
in barren conversation,
seeks itself by talking to itself:
what we were in years gone by
and what we would be in years to be.

The rearguard of the passers-by
lies under umbrellas
with bent ribs in
the lamp shade: the patron's
base, a dwelling
place without borders.
The cardboard on which they lie
may also be the roof felt.

Die Nebel-Patrouille
öffnet ihre Augen und
öffnet ihren Rachen und
schließt die hohle Hand, schlüpft unter
Untergrenzen durch, in
windstille Ecken, dann legt sich
Raureif auf die Haare,
Morgentau auf Plastiktüten.

Die Nachhut der Passanten zieht
hinter sich her die
Trümmer ihrer Zimmer an
Schnüren aufgereiht und
bleibt bis zum Morgen unter
Augustins Baldachin
in der ungeteilten
Obhut des Asphalts.

The fog patrol
opens its eyes,
opens its mouths and
closes the hollow of its hands, slips
through below lower limits,
into windless corners, then
frost lies on the hair,
morning dew on plastic bags.

The rearguard of the passers-by
pulls the wreckage
of its rooms behind it
strung on cords,
remains until morning
under Augustin's canopy
in the undivided custody
of the asphalt.

previously published in „Notre Dame Review", No. 42, Summer/Fall 2016

# DU HÄTTEST DIESE STADT BESUCHEN SOLLEN
## (für Konfliktforscher)

Du hättest diese Stadt besuchen sollen.
Hier auf der Ostseite des Marktplatzes,
gegenüber den Restaurants und Cafés,
stellten die jungen Damen klar: Wenn auf dem
Boden Glasscherben und Kronkorken herumlagen,
dann nur als Glitzerschmuck für ihren Laufsteg.
Sie waren oft ein wenig zu hübsch gekleidet
nur zum Einkaufen und viel zu schön für den Krieg.
Du hättest diese Stadt besuchen sollen,
weder mit dem Flugzeug noch mit dem Auto,
                    sondern zu Fuß,
um auf die Verkäufer einen Blick werfen zu können,
die auf dem Marktplatz laut ihre Waren anpriesen,
auf ihre leiseren, vorsichtigeren Kunden
und auf das Grün, das hier alles schmückte,
als Wasser noch leicht zu haben war.
Hättest Du diese Stadt besucht,
bevor der Tod sich hier eine Wohnung nahm,
hättest Du manchmal denken können,
dass kein Mensch etwas Böses denkt.

b. w.

## YOU SHOULD HAVE VISITED THIS CITY
(for peace researchers)


You should have visited this city.
Here on the eastside of the marketplace,
facing the restaurants and cafes, if glass shards
or flattened bottle caps littered the pavement,
the young ladies would make clear: this
was glittering decoration for their catwalk.
They were always a little too nicely dressed
just for shopping and much too beautiful for war.
You should have visited this city,
neither by plane, nor by car, but on foot,
to take a look at the street-vendors shouting their wares
on the marketplace and their silent customers
making their decisions deliberately.
When water was still easily available,
there was a lot more green around here.
Had you visited this city
before death took an apartment here,
sometimes you might have thought
no bad thoughts occurred to people's minds.

pto

Du hättest diese Stadt besuchen sollen,
als noch Frieden war.
Wenige Häuserblocks weiter saß eine alte Dame, die
jeden Tag die Tauben mit Mais und Sonnenblumenkernen
fütterte.
Stelle dir vor, Du wärest eines dieser Samenkörner.
Überlege, welche Chance du hättest, eine voll
ausgewachsene
Pflanze zu werden zwischen den Pflastersteinen –
so groß ungefähr ist die Chance, dass das,
was du hier tust, zu etwas Gutem führt.
Die alte Dame war immer noch da, als die Kinder
am selben Ort aus den ersten Ruinen Spielplätze machten,
sie stritt mit ihnen, sie sagte: „Was ihr tut, ist gefährlich",
die Kinder antworteten „Was du tust, ist
Verschwendung von Essen".
Du hättest diese Stadt besuchen sollen,
bevor der Tod sich hier eine Wohnung nahm,
du hättest diese Stadt besuchen sollen,
Bomberpilot im Himmel.

You should have visited this city
when peace still prevailed.
A few blocks further sat an old lady feeding
doves corn and sunflower seeds every day.
Imagine you were one of those seeds.
Consider your chance of becoming a fully grown plant
between the cobblestones on this square –
this equals the chance that what you
do here leads to something good.
The old lady was still sitting there when the children
were building their playgrounds out of the first ruins
on that place, always arguing with them,
she said what they were doing was dangerous,
they said what she was doing was a waste of food.
You should have visited this city,
before death took an apartment here,
you should have visited this city,
bomber pilot in the sky.

previously published in „Cincinnati Review", No 13/2, 2016

# DAS UNSICHTBARE BAND
(für Soziologen)

Auf jedem Feld
ein Forscher,
unter der Lupe das unsichtbare Band
für alle Dehnübungen
beim Tausch der Körperflüssigkeiten,
der Viren, der Symbole
und nicht zuletzt
der Bibliotheksausweise und
der Kopierkarten.

## THE INVISIBLE TIE
### (for sociologists)


On each field
a researcher,
under the microscope the invisible tie
for stretching exercises,
for the exchange of body
fluids, viruses, symbols
and last but not least
library cards and
copy cards.

## BERICHT VOM SCHEITERN DES VERSUCHS
## DER ABLEITUNG DES MORALISCH RICHTIGEN
## HANDELNS AUS DEN OBERSTEN PRÄMISSEN
## DIESES GEDICHTES

(für Soziologen)

Was noch so bunt emergiert,
wird nachher im Grauton kopiert.
Die Realität unterschätzt man,
Papp-Dinosaurier setzt man,
wo fern des Diskurses sie stehen:
in kaum mehr besuchte Museen.
Im Grand Hotel Abgrund nippt man
an Bloody Mary, dann kippt man
die Zweck-Rationalität vor
des idjologischen Überbaus Tor.
Banales derart zu verquasen,
erscheint wohl nicht jedem verblasen.

## REPORT ON THE FAILURE OF THE TRY
## TO DERIVE THE MORALLY RIGHT ACTION
## FROM THE SUPREME PREMISES
## OF THIS POEM
(for sociologists)


What emerged in full color one day
is subsequently copied in gray.
They act without remorse
far from the real discourse,
underestimate this reality,
clay dinosaur's banality
they put into museums. No one comes to see.
But here at the Grand Hotel Abyss they'll be
sipping on bloody Mary and then
the purpose-rationality is dumped again.
It seems blowing up common banalities
is one of their favorite modalities.

# DER TRICHTER
(für Pädagogen)

Wer als strenger Lehrer oder Richter
ein Löchlein bohrt in Schülerschädel
für den altbekannten Trichter,
der muss, ob nun bei Junge oder Mädel
wissen: dieser Plan gelingt nicht.
Das Loch fällt immer zu tief aus.
Wissen, so bewahrt, bleibt nicht dicht,
es läuft gleich unten wieder raus.


# PIMP DIE KERNKOMPETENZEN
(für Pädagogen)

Pimp' die Kernkompetenzen mit giga Pädagogika
zu Kompetenztänzen mit magna Didactica,
vergiss die Normschubladen, die tumben, die drögen,
wenn Du es nicht magst, wer soll es dann mögen.
Geh in den Stall, die Gesellen abschnallen,
Kompetenzgefälle wollen mit Donnerhall fallen,
ans Werk, das Fernziel, das Lernziel entstauben,
was Du selbst nicht glaubst, wer soll es Dir glauben.

## THE FUNNEL
(for pedagogues)


Who as a stringent, pungent teacher
drills a tiny hole or tunnel
into a student's skull to reach her
or him with the familiar funnel,
sees: this won't ever get right.
The hole's too deep again and so
it never will remain just quite tight,
the knowledge runs right out below.


## PIMP THE CORE COMPETENCIES
(for pedagogues)


Pimp the core competencies with giga pedagogics
to competence dances with magna didactics,
forget standard drawers now, make yourself understood,
cause if you don't like it yourself, who should.
Go to the stable, unbuckle the journeyman,
his skill gaps will fall with thunder then,
dust off the targets, don't let dust deceive you,
if you don't believe it, say, who's to believe you.

# NACHGEFORMTE STAATSGEBILDE
(für Politikwissenschaftler)

Manche kriegen beim Brennen Risse:
Auf der Arbeitsplatte
werden Staatsgebilde nachgeformt,
Kollektive und Systeme,
zwischen Bhagwan und Bakunin,
zwischen Herrn Rossi und Rousseau,
bei Ost-West, Nord-Süd,
Nahost, Feldpost, „oben" und „unten",
links, rechts, oben drüber und unten durch,
zwischen Morgenland und Abendland,
Käsebrot, Wurstbrot und Tofu.
Auch wenn im Chaos der Verwirbelungen
die großen Ströme sichtbar werden:
Nachträglich weiß man am Besten,
wo Prävention sinnvoll gewesen wäre.
Es würde aber auch schon helfen,
wenn ein HNO-Arzt den Leuten
mal die Ohren frei blasen würde.

## EMULATED STATE FORMATIONS
(for political scientists)


Some get cracks in the kiln:
On the countertop, state formations are emulated,
collectives and systems,
between Bhagwan and Bakunin,
between Mr. Rossi and Rousseau,
east-west, north-south.
the Middle East, field post,
upper and lower crust,
left, right, top and bottomless,
between East and West,
cheese sandwich, sausage sandwich, tofu.
Although the large streams are visible
in the chaos of turbulences:
Subsequently one knows best
where prevention would have been useful.
But it would already help
if otolaryngologists would
perform more earwax removals.

## MISS-ETAT

(für Wirtschaftswissenschaftler)

Dies ist die Prognosenmanufaktur,
hier die Theoriensortimente.
So wird der Wirtschaft ein Horoskop erstellt,
der Pudding festgenagelt,
der Schweinezyklus geschlachtet und auf's
Monopol gebrochen.
Deregulation ist Generalamnesie, fein heraus
aus der Krise geschrieben.
Die Prognose verändert ihren Gegenstand,
nur dass Abschaum fast immer
schön oben schwimmt.

## BUDGET LOST
(for economists)


This is the manufactory for forecasts,
here are the theory assortments.
They will create a horoscope for the economy,
the pudding gets nailed to the wall,
the monopole gets broken,
the pork cycle gets slaughtered.
Deregulation is general amnesty.
They try to write themselves out of the crisis.
The prognosis changes its object,
just that scum almost always
floats on the surface nicely.

# BÄRENHATZ
### (für Wirtschaftswissenschaftler)

Der Vorstandsvorsitzenden-Fritzen
chrom-blitzende Flitzer flitzen,
bis sie im Kurvensatz patzen:
Börsenplatz-Götzen platzen,
wenn Bärentatzen sie ritzen,
Wetteinsätze zerschlitzen.
Zerfetztes im Flattersatz:
statt Bodenschatz Bodensatz.
Protzer-Junkies mit Schlitzen
von leeren Geldspritzen.
Börsenplatz-Schnuckiputz
träumt vom Vollstreckungsschutz.
Der Aufsichtsratsvorsitz-Fritz
kotzt aus dem Schleudersitz.

## BEAR HUNT

(for economists)


The CEO-guys let their chrome-flashing
cans whizz around until they
mess up the curve set:
These tin gods of the stock
exchange center burst when
the bear claws scratch them,
wagers get shredded.
Residuum instead of gold.
Swanking junkies with slots
from empty cash infusions.
Stock exchange-sweetie pie
dreams of a stay of execution.
The chairman of the supervisory board
pukes out of the ejection seat.

# SEITENSTICHWORTE
(für Sportwissenschaftler)

Die Hammerweitwerfer drehen die Dinger,
mit drillenden Pillen ein Hürdenhochspringer,
für rege Generationen Regeneration
und Seitenstichworte für Dehnreflexion,
für Hängetrauma, Ermüdungsfraktur
und (in Majuskeln) die Muskulatur.
Bei schwankender Motivation dreiste Sprüche,
bei Einbruch der Leistung durch drei Leistenbrüche,
Massage an tiefen Gefäßinnenwänden,
um nach dem Warm-up das Cool-down zu spenden.

Auch Tieftaucher trifft mal der Mann mit dem Hammer.
Als Hochstapler füllt er die Doppelherzkammer,
mit Höhenflugkrankheit in den Überdrucksack,
das Herzminutenvolumen als Rucksack.
Auf die Boxernase nun das Nasenpflaster,
am Tennisarm vorne die Hand voller Zaster.
Bei klarem Ergebnis des nötigen Dopingtests,
das keinerlei Raum mehr für gnädiges Coping lässt,
ist Sportwort wohl Wortsport, ihr lustigen Sportschlümpfe,
schafft anderswo Fitness und reicht mir die Stützstrümpfe.

## STITCH CATCH WORDS
(for sport scientists)


These hammer throwers, they throw their things uphill,
a hurdler on treadmills may take thrilling pills still.
Then regeneration for all generations
and catch words for their muscle's smooth relaxation
for suspension trauma, and then for stress fracture
for the speaking muscles who will manufacture
perky patters now to give them their ration
in case of a faltering goal-motivation.
Massage of vascular angular inner walls,
to relaxedly cool down after the warm-up calls.

Sometimes deep diver's high hopes just lose glamour,
finally hit by the man with the hammer.
Use the Gamow bag for soaring disease.
Boxers need nasal strip's help not to wheeze.
The sport word is word sport, last whistles although
these tennis elbows have hands full of dough.
There is no more room for gracious coping
in case of clear results when they test for doping.
Give me support socks, you funny sport Smurf,
just don't create fitness down here on my own turf.

**2**

# Geist und Kunst /
# Spirit and Arts

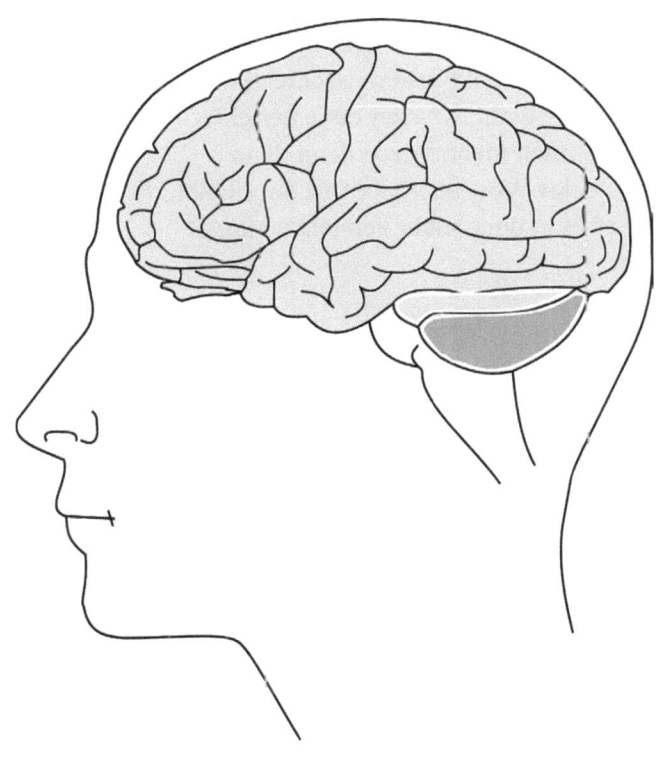

## KONSTRUKT UND KONSTRUKTION
(für Philosophen)

Zwei Philosophen sitzen im Lenz
unter des Kirschbaumes Seinsevidenz.
Sie legen Ideeneier, nesten und brüten,
und auch der Kirschbaum treibt typische Blüten.
Nun sagt der eine: „Das, was ich spreche,
kannst Du natürlich niemals verstehen.
Nicht weil ich mich zu behaupten erfreche,
Du würdest hirnlos durchs Dasein gehen.
Der radikale Konstruktivist,
der die Welt idiosynkratisch erfasst,
stellt fest, dass Verstehen unmöglich ist,
weil kein Konstrukt je zum anderen passt."
Der zweite bejaht, was der erste berichtet
und fragt auch nicht, wieso denn dann
der erste das Wort überhaupt an ihn richtet,
wenn er es ja doch nicht verstehen kann.

b. w.

## CONSTRUCT AND CONSTRUCTION
(for philosophers)


Under the existence evidence of the cherry tree,
two philosophers are talking intensely.
They sit there, develop ideas, nest and breed
and the vernal cherry tree also blossoms, indeed.
One of them utters: „You'll see there's no way
to really make you understand what I say.
Not because I presume to assume that your brain
is not capable of it or that you're insane –
constructivism, understood radically,
shows we grip the world idiosyncratically,
understanding's impossible, this will show,
no construct fits the other, constructivists know."
The second's affirmative, fortifies his ally,
doesn't ask himself or the other one why
these words are directed at him with no chance
that he ever listens and understands.

pto

Während die beiden so reden und nicken,
lässt sich, von ihnen bald ganz unbeachtet,
oben am Himmel ein Großflugzeug blicken,
das Menschen und Waren nach Bali verfrachtet.
Die, die das Flugzeug dereinst konstruierten,
waren in vierzehn Nationen gruppiert
und mit schon ziemlich stark spezialisiertem
Wissen und Werkzeugbestand ausstaffiert.
Sie sprachen in zwölf Dialekten und Sprachen,
sie stammten aus elfeinhalb Fachbereichen,
und verstanden sich so, dass die Flügel nie brachen
und stets von Frankfurt bis Bali reichen.
Das kümmert die beiden am Boden nicht
als radikale Konstruktivisten,
sie sitzen bei Denksport im Abendlicht,
um ohne Verstehen ihr Dasein zu fristen.

While both wonder what their words may imply,
unnoticed by them, up there in the sky,
an airplane appears that's about to transport
people and goods towards Bali's airport.
Those who constructed the airplane one day
came from fourteen nations, needless to say,
with specialized knowledge and artifacts.
They spoke fourteen languages / dialects,
came from more than eleven disciplines,
still people and goods always stay within
the plane to Bali or wherever it takes them
'cos the wings are stable enough, nothing breaks them.
This doesn't bother the two on the ground,
constructivists ignoring the plane's sight and sound,
they sit there alone in the evening light
to scrape their livings without an insight.

# GEDANKENEXPERIMENT

(für Philosophen)

Er jongliert mit Begriffen und wirft sie Dir zu,
er, der da geistig die Schranken nicht anerkennt.
Schließt er die Augen, so steigt sein IQ,
die Welt wird für ihn zum Gedankenexperiment.

Nacktere Tatsachen sind ihm verleidet,
was will man da schließlich auch noch abstrahieren.
Bestimmungen, äußeren, ist er entkleidet,
lässt sich durch die Wahrheit zu gar nichts verführen.

Als Dualist strebt er der geistigen Seite zu,
Körper versanken weit hinter dem Firmament,
schließt er die Augen, so steigt sein IQ,
das ist ein wahres Gedankenexperiment.

Will Überlegungen liegend bewegen,
induktiv schließt er im Zweifel auf Deduktion.
Wo genau ist er damit überlegen?
Weißt Du es nicht, dann sei sicher, er weiß es schon.

Er will das Wahre, das, was er das Schöne nennt,
Weises, Erkanntes, Ideen, die taugen,
das ist ein wahres Gedankenexperiment,
denkt er und denkt er und schließt seine Augen.

# THE GEDANKENEXPERIMENT
(for philosophers)


He juggles with concepts and throws them to you,
he, who denies mental barriers his consent,
he closes his eyes to increase his IQ,
the world is for him a gedankenexperiment.

For him, all these naked facts just interfere,
he asks what is left to abstract from, now, for him.
External conditions are sand in the gear,
he's not carried away by a truth that just bores him.

As a dualist, he leans towards the spiritual side,
physical bodies sink below the firmament,
when he closes his eyes, his IQ gets right,
the truth is for him a gedankenexperiment.

He considers the world while he's taking a rest,
inductively he concludes it's deduction.
Where exactly is he now superior at best?
If you do not know, hear his introduction.

He wants the truth and the beautiful, the good scent,
the sage, the detected, ideas that will rise,
this truly is a gedankenexperiment,
he thinks and he thinks and he closes his eyes.

## DEAR JURISPRUDENZ (BELEIDIGUNGSKLAGE)
(für Juristen)

Ich, sprich: also der Mandant, der eben Vorgenannte,
der amtlich und bekanntlich auf dem Amte darauf brannte,
gegen diese eklatanten, hirnverbrannten Dilettanten,
diese penetranten Querulanten und Pedanten,
die mich einen überspannten Ignoranten nannten,
ob leidiger Beleidigungen Klage zu erheben,
muss nun die beleidigendste Nachsagung erleben.
Ich sagte nie, man solle dem verklumpten alten Lumpen,
dem skrupellosen, skrupulösen Rüpel keinen pumpen,
ich sagte: „Nagel Deiner Frau die Scheuklappen zu,
der engbestirnten, kleinbehirnten Riesennilpferdkuh!"
Ich benenne das nun offiziell als schlichte Mängelrüge.
Weshalb ich meinesamtlich hiermit ebenso verfüge:
Es gesellt sich auch ganz ohne die gerichtliche Vereidigung
zur Beamten- hiermit die Selbständigenbeleidigung.
Das ist deutsche Rechtsbrechung und ohne Sack
                    und Hoden,
das sind Grundgesetze ohne Grund und ohne Boden,
das ist voller Mist, Sie Volljurist, Sie praller, voller,
Sie Verwalter eines Tollhauses, Sie selber Toller.

## DEAR JURISPRUDENCE (LIBEL SUIT)
### (for lawyers)


Me, the defendant, the pre-mentioned client,
unjustly insulted as being defiant,
officially I plead to punish this blatant,
inane and pedantic, pungent and latent
querulous idiot and dimwit, knucklehead.
Why punish me, you can punish him instead.
I just don't know why this numbskull hates me.
He called me "overstrained ignorant" lately.
I must experience sheer defamation.
I never threatened him with castration.
All I said was said smoothly, 'cause I never ever shout,
I said to this claggy old rascal, this lout:
„Go nail down your wife's pink veined blinders now,
her brain's just too small for a big hippo-cow!"
I will now declare this a simple complaint,
but one more insult and I'll give up restraint.
You lawn-gnome-lawyer, I dispose with unease:
This is a law of refraction without any testes.
You preside, sitting here on your bedpan,
over a madhouse, yourself being a madman.

## VOR'S GERICHT GESTELLT
### (für Juristen)

Sie haben eine Statue vor's Gericht gestellt,
macht'n Deal mit ihr, macht'n Deal mit ihr,
dem unbekannten V-Mann dazugesellt,
macht'n Deal, macht'n Deal, macht'n Deal,
als des ungekrönten Kronzeugen Segen,
macht'n Deal mit ihm, macht'n Deal mit ihm,
der muss Flugzeuge sprengen, der Glaubwürdigkeit wegen,
macht'n Deal, macht'n Deal, macht'n Deal.
Das ist, das weiß doch ich-weiß-nicht-wer,
klar wie Rechtsanspruch auch bei Linksverkehr,
macht'n Deal mit ihm, macht'n Deal mit ihm,
damit es was gibt zum Ausspionieren,
muss man's durch V-Mann-Lohn mitfinanzieren,
macht'n Deal mit ihm, macht'n Deal mit ihm.
Ist der Mann in Glaubwürdigkeitsnöten,
muss er halt mithelfen, Türken zu töten,
macht'n Deal, macht'n Deal, macht'n Deal.
Das dient doch alles dem höheren Ziel,
macht'n Deal, macht'n Deal, macht'n Deal.

## BEFORE THE COURT
### (for lawyers)


They have placed a statue before the court
make a deal with her, make a deal with her,
adjoined to the unknown informer's tort,
make a deal, make a deal, make a deal,
as a blessing of the uncrowned witnesses crown,
make a deal with him, make a deal with him.
To make the sceptical gangsters back down,
make a deal, make a deal, make a deal,
he has to rob and kill and blow up planes,
he has to sell some drugs and derail trains,
make a deal with him, make a deal with him.
That is, known to I-don't-know-who,
clear as your rights, in left-hand traffic, too,
make a deal, make a deal, make a deal.
So there is something to punish, something to pursue,
you have to finance it through the informer's due,
make a deal with him, make a deal with him,
this serves higher goals, as you will feel,
make a deal, make a deal, make a deal.

## RICHARD III

(für Theaterwissenschaftler)


Bevor irgendwer eine Vorstellung hat:
Beleuchters Lampenfieber
ob eines Zwischenspiels mit dem Glühdraht,
wegen Spannungsanstiegs
mit sich selbst durchgebrannt.
Dunkelheit. Jemand schneuzt
sich laut in voller Deckung.
Spot an, Spot auf Richard III. In-Szene.
Seine Grande Dame auf der Drehbühne,
im brennenden Schleudersitz als Drama-Mama,
schiebt einen Schrei in die Geräuschkulisse.
Er will eine andere
unter dem Kostüm inspizieren.
Wandernieren auf
Wanderbühnen, Statistensterben.
Am Ende hauptlos:
ein Hauptdarsteller.


## BRETTER

(für Theaterwissenschaftler)


Mancher Theaterbesitzer,
mancher Veranstalter
versteht die Wendung
„Die Bretter, die die Welt bedeuten"
dahingehend, dass das
Publikum kommt,
um seine Bretter zu besichtigen.


66

## RICHARD III

(for theatre scholars)


Before anyone has an idea:
Illuminator's stagefright
because of an interlude with the filament,
that blows because of the voltage rise
(causing darkness), echoed by someone who blows
his nose loudly under cover.
Spot on, spot on Richard III. In scene.
His Grande Dame on the revolving stage,
in the burning hot seat as a drama mama
she pushes a scream into the background
noise. He wants to inspect another one
under the costume.
Floating kidneys on
travelling theatre stages, extras are dying.
Headless at the end:
a headliner.


## BOARDS

(for theatre scholars)


Some theater owners
/some operators
understand the phrase
„The boards that mean the world"
to the extent that the
audience comes
to visit their boards.

## DIE ANHÄNGER DES KULTES VERSTÄNDIGEN SICH FREI VON SACHARGUMENTEN AUF DES-SEN OBJEKT     (für Literaturwissenschaftler)

Preisverleihung. Scheinwerfer an.
Da prangt er. Tribut:
Bücklinge in Dosen werden
angeliefert, Hofknickse als Lesezeichen,
Reputation auf repeat,
abgeschossene Vögel.
Leumund in aller Munde,
sie stoßen ihm ins Horn.
Chapeau, Claqueure, frenetische Frettchen,
Scharlatane in Scharen,
an die große Glocke zu hängen,
ans Bundesverdienstkreuz zu nageln!
Auf offener Bühne: Durchbruch
des Dachdeckers,
Stockwerk für Stockwerk,
als Kellergeschoss.

## THE DEVOTEES OF THE CULT AGREE ON ITS OBJECT FREE OF FACTUAL ARGUMENTS
(for literary scholars)


Award presentation ceremony. Headlights on.
There he flaunts. Tribute:
Canned kippers are delivered,
curtseys as bookmarks,
reputation on repeat,
shot birds.
Renown on everyone's lips,
they take the same lines.
Kudos, hired applauders, frenetic ferrets,
charlatans come in flocks,
to be hanged on a lantern,
to be nailed to the Grand Cross of Merit!
On the open stage: Breakthrough
of the roofer,
floor by floor,
down to the basement.

# GOETHE-GENERATOR
## (für Literaturwissenschaftler)

Germanistische Geisterbeschwörung,
gelegentlich geistige Gleichgewichtsstörung,
gelegentlich Gurke, Gehirnerweichung,
gelegentlich Granate, geniale Gleichung,
Glücksgriffe, großartig gesponnen, gelungen
gegen Geklapper-Geplapper, gewunden, gezwungen,
grundgescheiter Geniestreiche Glorienschein
gegen geistigen Gallenstein, glanzloses Gänseklein,
günstigenfalls gut: Gedankengeranke
gegen glanzlos-gelangweiltes, graues Gezanke,
großer Gedanken generöse Gelassenheit
gegen Geier-Geleier, Gefasel, Geschwätzigkeit,
gerne genommen: großer Geister Gabe,
gelegentlich Geraune, gymnasiales Gehabe,
gesteigerte Geberlaune, graziöser Glimmer
gegen gelinde gesagt grauenvolles Gewimmer.
Gemunkel, Gemurmel, Gelehrte gestehen:
Geheimnis-Geknister: gerne gesehen.
Glücksfall: Goethe-Generatoren geraten,
geringstenfalls Goethes Gedärme – gebraten.

## METAKRITIK SONETTE RELATIVIERENDER
## AUTOTHEMATIK (für Literaturwissenschaftler)

Ein Sonett über solche Sonette zu dichten,
die selbst wiederum nur Sonette behandeln,
das ließe Dich quasi im Hamsterrad wandeln.
Ich bitte Dich also, darauf zu verzichten.

Das Spiegelbildlein Deines Nabels zu spiegeln
nervt Leser zu Tode, es ist wie ein Fluch.
Man riecht auch schon quasi den Modergeruch.
Lass uns diese Türe für immer verriegeln.

Das führt nur dahin, dass man es übertreibt.
Über's Dichten zu dichten – nun, das lasse bleiben,
jede Metadichtebene wird es verschlimmern.

Denn wer hierbei schreibende Schreiber beschreibt,
die selbst grade über das Schreiben schreiben,
darf über der Leser Gewimmer nicht wimmern.

## DICHTEN IN ISOLIEREND SPRACHE
(für Linguisten)

Du denken, Du grade, ich denken: Du krumm.
Du in mein Ohr gestern labern viel dumm.
Du ganz verblöden wenn Du niemals gehen raus,
nur Du hier sitzen – es morgen so sehen aus.
Sprachtyp viel interessant, nun, so Du sagen.
Ich glauben Du gern, aber ich wollen fragen:
Wann Du wollen sehen Leben plus Wirklichkeit?
Du sitzen in Bibliothek, haben nein viel Zeit.
Du lernen aus Buch was Du glauben sein echt,
nicht reden mit viel Mensch von anders Geschlecht.
Du lernen aus viel Buch von viel Sprachtyp nur.
Du besser auch reden mit anders Kultur.
Du lieben viel Buchstabe, sehen viel Wand.
Aber anders Geschlecht sein auch interessant.

# WRITING IN ISOLATING LANGUAGE
## (for linguists)

You thinking, you even, I more thinking, you bent.
In my ear often you babbling ignorant.
You all going gaga if you never going out,
you sitting there always – tomorrow not any doubt.
Language type much interesting, so now saying you.
I believing you liking this, but I wanting asking, too:
When wanting seeing life, seeing reality?
You sitting in library, outside being absentee.
You learning from book, much time having not,
not talking to people of different gender a lot.
You learning a lot about language types only.
Not talking with culture other, being lonely.
You loving a lot of letter, seeing a lot of wall.
But other sex being more interesting after all.

## METALYRISCHES PLÄDOYER FÜR HUMAN-ÜBERSETZUNG

(für Übersetzungswissenschaftler)

Original: LÄDIERTER LATTENROST

Ludwig liebte Lottes Lüsternheit,
Lockender Locken Liebenswürdigkeit.
Lotte liebte Ludwig leichtberitten.
Ludwigs Lagerstättes Latten litten.
Lottes lebensfrohe Liebeslust
Lädierte leider Ludwigs Lattenrost.
Lottes liebster Ludwig lachte lediglich.
Lädierte Latten? Lamentieren? Lächerlich.
Liebkoste lieber Lottes Leberflecken,
Liebte lückenloses Lendenlecken.
Lothar leimte Ludwigs Lattenrost lattenweise.
Lotte leckte lieber Ludwigs Latte leise.

Google-Sprachtools-Übersetzung: LÄDIERTER SLAT RUST

Ludwig loved plumb bob width units Lüsternheit,
Luring curls kindness.
Lotte loved Ludwig easy-mounted.
Ludwig Lagerstättes slats suffered.
Plumb bob width unit life-glad dear desire
Lädierte unfortunately Ludwig's slat rust.
Plumb bob width unit dearest Ludwig laughed only.
Lädierte slats? Lamentieren? Ridiculously.
Dear-cost dear plumb bob width unit liver marks,
Complete Lendenlecken loved.
Lothar glued Ludwig's slat rust lattenweise.
Lotte licked dear Ludwig's slat quietly.

b. w.

74

## METALYRICAL PLEA FOR HUMAN TRANSLATI-ON

(for translation scholars)

ORIGINAL: LETTERS

Letter landscapes, lovesick letters,
lazy, lavish, lipstick letters,
letter litter, limelight letters,
loose-leaf, loose-lipped landslide letters,
linking life's lanes limitlessly,
labelling lives luminously.
Livid legislator's letters,
lucid liberator's letters,
legitimizing liberty.
Lee's longhand lacks lucidity.

GOOGLE TRANSLATION INTO GERMAN: BRIEFE

Schreiben Landschaften, Liebeskummer Briefe,
faul, verschwenderisch, Lippenstift Briefe,
Brief Wurf Rampenlicht Briefe,
Lose-Blatt, lose Lippen Erdrutsch Briefe,
Verknüpfung von Lebensspuren grenzenlos,
Kennzeichnung lebt leuchtend.
Livid Gesetzgebers Briefe,
luziden Befreier Briefe,
Legitimierung Freiheit.
Lees Langschrift fehlt Klarheit.

pto

Google-Sprachtools-Rückübersetzung: LÄDIERTER
LATTE-ROST

Ludwig liebte Lotbreite Maßeinheiten Lüsternheit
und lockte Wellungen Freundlichkeit an.
Lotte liebte einfach-angebrachten Ludwig.
Ludwig Lagerstättes Latten litten.
Lotbreite Maßeinheit Leben-frohen lieben Wunsch
Lädierte leider Ludwigs Latterost.
Lotbreite Maßeinheit liebster Ludwig lachte nur.
Lädierte Latten? Lamentieren? Lächerlich.
Lieb-Kosten liebten liebe Lotbreite Maßeinheit
Lebermarkierungen, komplettes Lendenlecken.
Lothar klebte Latte-Rost lattenweise Ludwigs.
Lotte leckte Latte lieben Ludwigs ruhig.

GOOGLE TRANSLATION BACK INTO ENGLISH:
LETTERS

Write landscapes, lovelorn letters,
lazy, wasteful, Lipstick Letters,
Letter throw spotlight letters,
Loose-leaf, loose lips landslide letters,
Combination of traces of life limitless,
Labeling lives bright.
Livid legislature letters,
lucid liberator letters,
Legitimization of freedom.
Lees longhand lack clarity.

## MIT DEM BLASROHR IN DIE ZEITSCHRIFT
(für Ethnologen)

Mungo Park fährt, das ist sein Traum,
zum Begräbnis der Sardine
auf der Isar in nem Einbaum,
trägt die Tracht mit saurer Miene,
nimmt zum flüssigen Flektieren
Schluckbildchen aus alten Zeiten,
will mit Sprachen fusionieren,
eins mit allen Wirklichkeiten,
untersucht mit X Sensorien
vom Meer verbliebne Lachen
auf den weiten Territorien
von ausgestorbnen Sprachen,
zieht mit Tribes aus Ostwestfalen,
schreibt zu Voodoo eine Streitschrift,
will mit Liebesdienst bezahlen,
schießt mit Blasrohr in die Zeitschrift,
spricht im fernen Yokohama
gerne von den Abenaki,
spricht die Dame nur Kunama,
teilt er mit ihr seine Kaki.

b. w.

# INTO THE MAGAZINE BY BLOWPIPE
(for ethnologists)


Mungo Park goes, that is his dream,
to the burial of the sardine
on the Isar's vigorous stream,
ships a dugout through the smoke screen,
wants to merge himself with words,
unite with all realities
and with all inflecting nerds,
studies puddles where there once were seas.
Schluckbildchen from ancient times
he takes for vague advantages,
within vast territories he climbs
the heights of extinct languages
where testimonia are still rife,
with X sensoria never seen
he wants to feel, see all of life,
shoots right into the magazine
with a blowgun made of bamboo,
takes love labor for his bribes,
writes polemics about Voodoo,
moves with East Westphalian tribes.

pto

Er erkundet die Gefühle,
eins mit diesem Weltgewühle,
will vom Leben alles sehen,
zieht Kulturkreise beim Gehen,
trägt die Glut in ein Museum,
sucht das indische Te Deum,
tanzt auf Digeridoo-Klänge
und auf Ahnenkult-Gesänge,
will Schamanen ihre Fabelwesen
aus dem Ohr und aus dem Nabel lesen,
Etnologi bei den Kogi,
*dân tộc học* bei den Modoc,
bleibt er immer لم عِ ناس جَالأ,

ɯqqɯqɲɯqʕɯ, জাতিতত্ত্বিক,

માનવજાતના વિજ્ઞાનનો અભ્યાસી,

मानवजाति विज्ञानी, 民族学者,

ವంశశాస్త్రజ్ఞ మానవజాతి శాస్త్రవేత్త,

ชาติพันธุ์วิทยา.

In distant Yokohama,
he talks of the Abenaki
if the lady speaks Kunama,
it's with her he shares his Kaki.
He sings the Indian Te Deum,
carries embers to museums,
to didgeridoo sounds he dances
an ancestor worship chant, he chants it,
wants to find mythical creatures
within shaman's body features,
Etnologi with the Kogi,
*dân tộc học* with the Modoc,
he always remains   الأج ناس ع لم,

ɯqqɯqɲɯqɐɯ, জাতিতত্ত্বিক,

માનવજાતના વિજ્ઞાનનો અભ્યાસી,

मानवजाति विज्ञानी, 民族学者,

ವಂಶಶಾಸ್ತ್ರಜ್ಞ మానవజాతి శాస్త్రవేత్త,

ชาติพันธุ์วิทยา.

## DER BUSCH DER ERKENNTNIS
(für Theologen)

Sie gehen mit Gottes Wort
in den Copyshop,
die auf den Spuren der Schamanen
über Runen lehnen,
wiegen den Stein der Weisen,
den keltischen Ahnenkult.

Kreuzritter im Lesesaal
befragen die Inquisition,
Papstsimulation im Reagenzglas,
religiöse Ekstase mit Elektroden,
Schisma im Prisma
und den Heiligenschein.

Ein Schamane hält
einen Powerpoint-Vortrag.
Jetzt wird Gottesfurcht buchstabiert
in verstorbenen Sprachen,
sachlich zergliedert die
Andacht und Demut.

Brennt der Busch der Erkenntnis
im Vorlesungssaal?
Einer folgt der inneren Stimme hinaus,
meditiert auf eigene Rechnung
und schaut dann tief ins Glas
zum Urgrund des Seins.

## THE BUSH OF KNOWLEDGE
(for theologians)


They go with God's Word
to the copy shop,
they, leaning over the runes
on the trail of the shaman,
weigh the philosopher's stone,
the Celtic ancestor's worship.

Crusaders in the reading room
consult the Inquisition,
Pope simulation in a test tube,
religious ecstasy with electrodes,
schism in the prism
and the halo.

A shaman holds a
PowerPoint lecture.
Now the fear of God is
spelled in late languages,
reverence and humility
are dissected soberly.

Does the bush of knowledge
burn in the lecture hall?
One follows the inner voice,
meditates on his own account
and then looks deep into the glass
to the ultimate ground of being.

## SISYPHOS' STARALLÜREN
### (für Theologen)

Sisyphossens Sonnenbrillen
signalisierten Siegeswillen.
Sein Sandstein sauste, suchte Senken.
Satans Sicherheitsbedenken:
„Solch Sakrileg, solch Saufbold, solch
selbstgerechter Sittenstrolch,
sein Sülzkopf: satter Sünden Sitz!"
Sisyphos soff Slibowitz,
sagte säuselnd seinethalben:
„Satan soll sich selber ... salben."
Satan sagte: „Sisyphos!
Solch Starallüren – sittenlos!
Sisyphossi sabotiert.
Sanktion: sofortig suspendiert!
So subversiv, so skrupellos!"
„Super!", sagte Sisyphos.
Sein Sujet seit seinem Siegen:
singen, swingen, segelfliegen.

## SISYPHUS' STARDOM

(for theologians)


Sisyphus' sunglasses signalize:
Sisyphus schedules some surprises.
Sandstones swish, searching sinks.
Satan says: „Such stardom stinks.
Such sacrilege, such scallywag,
Sisyphus' signings, sorrows sag!"
Sisyphus sipped slivovitz,
said: „Screwy sicko Satan spits."
Satan said: „Sisyphus' suppuration,
self-satisfaction, self-stimulation.
Sisyphus sabotaged sacrilegiously,
sanction: suspending Sisyphus sagaciously,
searching scareheads, selfish squarehead!"
„Self-sufficiency! Super!", Sisyphus said.
Sisyphus' subject since such salvation:
singing, swinging, sweet sensations.

## AUS EINER UNTERGEGANGENEN REPUBLIK
(für Theologen)

Welchen Teil des Tempels
für die Götter
soll man abschließen um sie
zu schützen
vor dem Verfall des Glaubens
bevor der eine
kommt und alles an sich reißt

## MESSAGE FROM AN EXTINCT REPUBLIC
(for theologians)


Which part of the temple to the Gods
should we close to
protect them from
the decay of faith
before the One
comes and takes
everything for himself


previously published in in: Jonathan MS Pearce (Editor): Filling The Void:
A Selection Of Humanist And Atheist Poetry, Onus Books, 2016

## STRASSENZÜGE HABEN FALTEN
(für Historiker)

Straßenzüge haben Falten.
Dies war Ruine, das vergittert,
Zeugen alter Kriegsgewalten
und von Schüssen aufgesplittert.
Unter Wurzeln alter Bäume,
zwischen Steinen alter Mauern,
Nachtmar, unerfüllte Träume,
ausgespült von Regenschauern.
In der Stadt finden sich Spuren
von Menschen, die verschwanden
nach des Teufels Partituren
und von Menschen, die sich fanden.
Häuser aus Vergangenheiten.
Der Asphalt besteht aus Lagen,
Schicht für Schicht auf alten Zeiten,
unterm Einband aufzuschlagen,
und man kann Hilferufe lesen.
Tiefer Frost brachte die Risse
in die Mauern, zwischen Wesen.
Dann verschob sich die Kulisse.
Eine Abfolge von Bildern.
Jede Mischmasch-Häuserzeile
hilft, die Abfolge zu schildern,
liefert dafür Puzzleteile.
Zieh den Vorhang ganz zur Seite,
wisch die Abgasspuren fort
und der Blick geht in die Weite,
tausend Plätze, nur ein Ort.

## STREETS HAVE FOLDS
(for historians)


Streets have wrinkles.
This was a ruin, that was enclosed,
witness of old war powers
and fragmented by shots.
Below roots of old trees,
between stones of old walls,
nightmares, unfulfilled dreams,
rinsed by the rain.
In the city, there are traces
of people who disappeared
according to the devil's instructions,
and of people who found each other.
Houses from different pasts.
The asphalt is composed of layers,
layer by layer from ancient times
to read, below the cover,
and you can read cries for help.
Deep freeze brought the cracks
in the walls and between beings.
Then the setting shifted.
A succession of frames.
Each mishmash row of houses
helps to describe the sequence,
provides pieces for the puzzle.
Pull away the curtain entirely,
wipe off the traces of exhaust
and the view goes to the distance,
a thousand locations, just one place.


accepted by the Ghent Review, Belgium, 2017

## UNTER DEM KELLER
### (für Archäologen)

Am Tatort befindlich:
Ein Maulwurf im Menschenpelz
grüßt recht verbindlich,
gräbt sich durch Stein und Fels,
Türme von Babylon
unter dem Keller
sind bald verkabelt, schon
gräbt es sich schneller,
Funde im Angesicht,
schaufelnd die Pfoten,
quer durch die Lavaschicht,
ins Reich der Toten,
die nach ihm riefen,
birgt sie dann Stück für Stück.
Würmer, die schliefen,
bleiben verdutzt zurück.

## BELOW THE BASEMENT
(for archaeologists)


Located below the block:
A mole digs in human skin,
scrabbling through stone and rock,
he greets with a friendly grin,
digs faster and faster,
Babylon's towers wait
here below the plaster,
they'll reach a wired state.
He's got finds in the face,
paws paddle in mummy's bed,
all through the lava's grace,
into the realm of the dead
who call while he's creeping,
get recovered relaxedly.
Worms who were sleeping
stay back perplexedly.

# TIEFLANDTAUCHER

(für Archäologen)

Der Tieflandtaucher Metalldetektoren,
Sehhilfe eines vom Tageslicht Blinden,
schlagen sich Tag und Nacht um die Ohren,
an Ufern entlang, bis sie Grabhügel finden.
In jeder Erdreichsstadt, in die der Lichtschein kam,
schmücken sich Tote für Museumsbühnen,
in Troja, in Akkad, in Pompeji und Elam.
Menschen, Gedränge an ihren Vitrinen.
Was Ratten und Würmern und Rostfraß nicht schmeckte,
das kann den Zahn der Zeit selbst noch beschönigen.
Und auch die Herrschaft des Manns, der's bezweckte.
Verneigt Euch vor Künstlern, nicht vor den Königen.

## DEEP LAND DIVER
(for archaeologists)


The deep land divers' metal detectors,
vision aid for those blinded by daylight,
pull an all-nighter, pull an all-dayer
along the shore until they find barrows.
In each reilluminated soil city,
the dead adorn themselves for museum stages,
in Troy, in Akkad, in Pompeii and Elam.
A crowd surges at their showcases.
What didn't taste rats and worms and corrosion,
can now palliate the ravages of time.
And the reign of the man who aimed at this.
Bow before artists, not before kings.

# BERGUNG RÜCKWÄRTS

(für Archäologen)

Man hatte die versunkene, die
Unterwasserstadt, geborgen und mit Hilfe
der aufwändigsten und modernsten Verfahren
auf trockenem Grund neu platziert.
Dort sollte sie in all ihrer Pracht
unzählige Bewunderer finden,
ihre Rätsel offenbaren,
von ihren Bewohnern erzählen.

Dann allerdings ereignete sich ein
unvorhergesehenes Unglück,
als ob ein Fluch aus der Zeit der
Entstehung sich erfüllt hätte,
ausgesprochen, um die Bergung
zu vermeiden und das Rätsel zu wahren.
Man musste die Stadt eilig
an ihren Ursprungsort zurück verfrachten.

Zu groß wäre sonst das Drama geworden,
das Mutter aus der Angelegenheit machte,
als sie, zur Besichtigung an
den neuen Standort auf dem
Boden des Kinderzimmers geladen,
das Badewasser bemerkte, das aus den
Zwischenräumen der Legosteine
sickerte.

## REVERSE RECOVERY
(for archaeologists)


One had recovered the sunken
underwater city and repositioned it
on dry ground using the most sophisticated
and advanced methods.
There, the city with all its glory
was supposed to find countless admirers,
to reveal its mystery and to
tell of its inhabitants.

Then, however, an unforeseen calamity occurred,
as if a curse from the time of emergence
would have fulfilled – pronounced
to avoid the salvage and preserve the mystery.
He had to bring the city
back to its original location.

Mother would otherwise have made too big
a drama out of the matter when she,
being invited to visit the new location
on the floor of the nursery, noticed the
bath water that seeped from the
interstices of the Lego bricks.


previously published in "the 7th Quarry", UK, 2015

# FREITREPPE IN DEN HIMMEL
## (für Architekten)

Er setzt mit an Linien entlang sich bewegenden
Händen gedachte Gebäude in Gegenden,
Adams gemauerte Rippe in Segelform
auf Tiefbau, Zentralbau, Massivbau in Kegelform.
Er will Fundamente nach unten verjüngen,
die städtische Landschaft mit Bleistiften düngen,
rasch filetiert er das Konversions-Areal
horizontal, nach Plan, filigran, vertikal.

Er, der im Geist Land- und Stadtschaft durchdringt,
in kubischen Winkel-Gedanken versinkt,
träumt schon im Stahlbetonhäusergewimmel
von einer Freitreppe bis in den Himmel,
setzt auf die imaginärste Skyline
schon den gedachten Schlussstein aus Gussstein,
läuft den Entwurf entlang zur Kolonnade.
Für ihn ist der Berg Tunnel-Außenfassade.

## PERRON TO THE SKY
(for architects)


He sets imaginary buildings into areas
with hands moving along lines,
Adams brick rib in sail shape, decorates
concrete constructions, central structures concretely.
He wants to rejuvenate foundations downwards,
fertilize the urban landscape with pencils,
quickly he fillets the conversion area
horizontally, according to plan, vertically.

He who penetrates rural and urban shank in mind
sinks into cubic angle thoughts
within the reinforced concrete houses throng
dreaming of a stairway to heaven.
Then he sets the imaginary capstone of cast stone
to another imaginary skyline,
running the draft along the colonnade.
For him the mountain is the tunnel's external facade.

accepted by the Ghent Review, Belgium, 2017

## Das ist nicht REAL. Das ist BARCELONA.
### (für Architekten)

Du tauchst auf aus dem Meer, hinein in die Stadt.
In Fassaden setzen sich die Wellen fort.
Ein Guckloch in die Gegenwelt, abgeschrägt,
auf dem Weg vom Diesseits ins Jenseits
machst du hier einen Schlenker.
Gibt es überhaupt eine andere Stadt?
Es ist alles eine Strömung, von Wirbeln verziert,
zwischen Maremagnum, La Rambla,
Plaça de Catalunya, Casa Milà, Palau Güell.
Das genügt sich selbst:
Casa Batlló, Park Güell – Sagrada Familia:
Geschmolzene Kerze, Barcelona
macht aus der Sonne einen Scheinwerfer,
ragt in den Himmel über dem Meer.
Anderswo bestenfalls
interessante Varianten von Bekanntem.
Stadt für Stadt ein Pfostenschuss.
Aber das ist nicht REAL. Das ist BARCELONA.
Gott blickt verwirrt und staunt
und möchte auch mal was erschaffen.

**This is not REAL. This is BARCELONA.**
(for architects)


You surface from the sea, dive into the city.
In façades, the waves continue.
A peephole into the counterworld, slanted,
on the way from this life to the hereafter,
you're making a detour here.
Is there another city at all?
It's all a flow, decorated by swirls,
between Maremagnum, La Rambla,
Placa Catalunya, Casa Mila, Palau Güell.
This is self-sufficient.
Casa Batlló, Park Güell – Sagrada Familia:
Melted candle, Barcelona
makes the sun a headlight,
protrudes into the sky over the sea.
Elsewhere, at best,
interesting variants of the familiar.
Town by town a shot against the bar.
But this is not REAL. This is BARCELONA.
God looks confused and amazed
and wants to create something sometimes, too.

# WELLEN KRÖNEN

(für Kunsthistoriker)

In skizzierte Objekte dringt Farbe ein,
bis Wind manche quer über die Leinwand hetzt.
Pinselstrich mauert die Kaimauer Stein für Stein.
Schaumkronen werden dem Wellengang aufgesetzt.
Dort wird die Leinwand mit Seetang bepflanzt,
liefern Farben statt Wasserdampf Schnüfflerware.
War der nicht kahl? Weil die Ölspur tanzt,
kriegt auch der Schädel gestrichene Haare.
Dann: Schwingungslinien ersetzen den Wellengang,
jetzt ist die Dreamachine Hüter des Schieferblaus,
einhundert Jahre lang immer der Form entlang,
dann das Ende der Leinwand,
darüber hinaus.

## CROWN THE WAVES
### (for art historians)


Colors penetrate sketched objects
until wind rushes some of them across the canvas.
Brushstrokes build the quay wall, stone by stone.
Whitecaps are placed on the swell.
The canvas is planted with seaweed,
some colors provide snoop goods instead of steam.
Wasn't he bald? Because the oil track dances,
his skull gets painted hair.
Then: vibrational lines replace the swell,
now the Dreamachine is guardian of the slate blue,
always along the shape for a hundred years,
then comes the end of the canvas,
it's continued beyond.

# TERPENTINA

(für Kunsthistoriker)


dreht eine Runde auf Papier
auf Terpentinserpentinen,
verrät mit keiner Miene Züge.
Zoom auf den Spion
mit Silberblicken:
Von Sporen-Jalousien
mit Eifersucht bewacht,
sprudeln aus Lichtquellen
kleine Kugelblitze.
Terpentina aus Tinkturkestan,
von Tarantino gestochen,
Glühbirne und Bratapfel
vergleicht sie mit dem Pinsel,
indem sie unsterbliche Überreste
unter dem Firnis hinterlässt.

## TURPENTINA

(for art historians)


goes for a spin on paper
on turpentine serpentines,
reveals no moves with her expression.
Zoom in on the spy
with silver eyes:
jealously guarded
by spore-blinds,
small ball lightning bubbles
out of light sources.
Turpentina from Tinkturkestan,
stung by Tarantino,
she compares light bulb
and baked apple with a brush
by leaving immortal remains
under the varnish.

## BODY ART

(für Kunsthistoriker)

Er gießt seine Warze
in Epoxidharze,
tritt Milchprodukte breit
und nennt's „Neo-Sachlichkeit",
tritt Milchprodukte klein
und nennt es dann „Food Design",
träumt vom großen Fluxus
und lebt seinen Luxus,
schreit: „Pudelnackt stehen –
das ist Neues Sehen!
Griffelkunst! Punzenstich!
Body Art nennt man mich!"

## BODY ART

(for art historians)


With epoxy resins of some sorts,
he plans to make some casts of his warts,
he tramples curd with creativity
and then calls it „New Objectivity“,
he tramples curd, then he enshrines it,
and photographs his „food design hit“,
he dreams of big Fluxus, he
sure lives his luxury,
he shouts: „Nakedness, that was all it took –
that is the new art, the newest look!
Look at the warts and the other parts!
Before I fall apart call me body art!“

# PIXELSCHICKSAL

(für Gestalter)

Was da kreucht und leuchtet,
funkt und flunkert und flimmert,
als Antipustelapostel
Tiefdruck und Hochglanz verziert,
auf digital frisierten Pix
schimärenhaft schimmert:
ein modelliertes Model
blinkt gezinkt, retuschiert.
Mit blonden Lendenblenden,
ohne Blutgerinnsel,
mit Zimtbaumrinde,
Zuckerguss versehen und bemalt,
steht Stretch-Tine Pastellmamsell
vom Pixelpinsel,
gesäuberte Lichtqualle,
fein getäfelt und verschalt.
Für den Bulimie-Bullenmarkt
säbelt die Nebelmaschine
erst alle Runzelknospen
mit dem Pixelbeil,
stretcht Tine dann auf Passung
mit der Stretchlimousine,
schiebt Stiefmutter Natur
fix ab aufs Altenteil
zu den Abstellgreisen,
auf Dekubitusmatten,
abseits des Scheins,
im Scheinwerferschatten.

## PIXEL POLITICS
(for designers)


See how it flimflams and shines,
fibs, flickers and glimmers,
anti-pimple-apostles deck
gravure and glossy print,
digitally doctored pics,
see how they shimmer
in a chimeric way,
see modeled models glint.
Stretch-Tine pastel-damsel,
without bruises she stands
within sugarcoating,
within cinnamon bark,
retouched by the pixel brush,
the queen of all brands,
pure damsel, sauce of light,
she is gift-wrapped, a spark.
For bulimia bull markets,
the fogger, unseen,
hacks all wrinkle-buds
with the pixel hatchet,
stretches Christine
to fit the stretch limousine,
pushes stepmother nature;
unable to stretch her,
to the senior siding,
on bedsore mats' side,
into spotlight shadows,
away from the light.

# KLANGFARBEN UND SCHALLQUELLEN
(für Musikwissenschafler)

Aufs Trommelfell fließen zum Grundschlag des Taktes
durch Hörmuscheln zwischen den Quarten und Quinten
die schnellen Synkopen des kommenden Aktes
zum Ort ihres Auftritts in Hirnlabyrinthen.

Der Gleichgewichtssinn will mit steppenden Füßen
sein Lob bis zu höheren Tönen verstimmen,
mit Ohren als Segel lässt er schön grüßen,
will er die Schallwellenberge erklimmen.

Pizzicato in Sätzen, die zugespitzt sitzen,
dann Tonsprung zur Sexte, zur siebten Septime,
als Ping-Pong des Klingklangs, als Zickzack der Blitze,
zu Klangfarben, Schallquellen, Terz und Dezime.

Neuronen-Bolero als Lohn macht die Party zur
Jagd, eine Note spürt das wohl mental schon,
Staccato, Vibrato, die Note auf Partytour
spritzt aus der Partitur, hin zum Zentralton.

Synapsen morsen ans Hörzentrum: Tangoschritt!
Cha cha cha heißt es in rhythmischer Rotation.
Ein vibrierender Hörnerv tanzt dann beim Fandango mit.
Die Noten als Boten der Toten, doch schon:

Hip Hop in Hit Clips als doppelter Kontrapunkt,
Ikonen sind raubkopiert, brutto wie netto,
wenn schon der Herzschlag im Rhythmus
        der Bassdrum funkt,
hat hier bestimmt wer'n Libretto in petto.

## TIMBRES AND SOUND SOURCES
(for musicologists)


Raw syncopations flow out of their stock
between fourths and fifths, to the beat of the clock,
pass earlobes, hit eardrum, keep finding their ways
to the place of their staging down there in the brain's maze.

When more fundamental bass resounds, it restarts,
use your ears as two sails, vibrating nerves send
                    their regards,
the senses of balance go dancing with quick feet,
the praise is transposed to the treetop tone's quick beat,

pizzicato in sets that do always sit pointedly,
a jump to the sixth, so it will swing anointedly,
a ping-pong of sing sound, a zigzag of lightning,
and then shuffle on, third and tenth become brightening.

Staccato, vibrato flow out of the disco's door,
a note is on party tour, injected from the score
towards the central tone, see how it bears the brunt
while neuron bolero makes dancing a nightlight hunt.

Morse code to the synapses: tango step, tango!
A nerve meanwhile dances like it's a Fandango.
Then cha cha cha, rhythmic rotation is steady.
Composers, some decomposed, greet us, already:

Hip hop and hit clips now serves us as counterpoints,
pirated pop icons, everyone moves their joints,
the rhythm of bass drums, it triggers the pop heartbeats,
surely they have life librettos to meet our needs.

# 3

# Natur / Nature

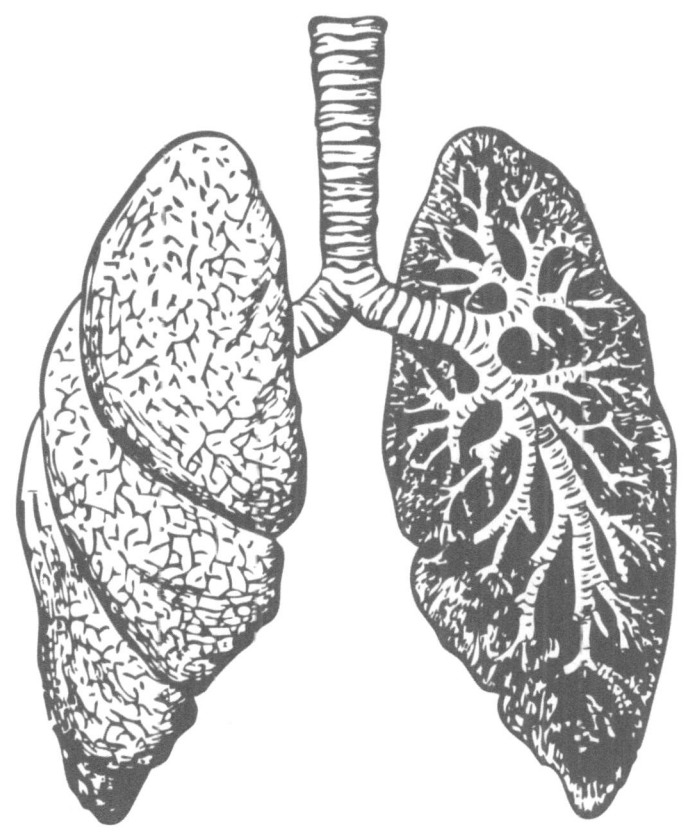

# BLITZEN APPLAUDIEREN

(für Meteorologen)

Komm, lass uns Blitzen applaudieren,
der beste Platz dafür ist hier,
und zuseh'n, was sie inszenieren
am Himmel über dir und mir.
Sieh im Wind die dunklen Wälder,
die sich wiegen, Baum zu Baum.
Noch elektrischere Felder
als diese findest du wohl kaum.
Lass uns den Wolkenberg studieren,
vom Faradayschen Käfig aus,
und wenn die Blitze imponieren,
dann spenden wir Applaus.
Hör, wie die Wolken sich entspannen,
zu Regentrommeln auf dem Dach,
wie sie Spannungen verbannen.
Tropfen verbinden sich zum Bach.
Sieh draußen ferne Linien rasen.
Dann sind die Donner schnell verklungen.
Die Ladungen sind weggeblasen
mit Lippen und mit Engelszungen.

# APPLAUDING FLASHES
### (for meteorologists)

Come, let us applaud flashes,
the best place for it is here,
and see what they stage
in the sky above you and me.
See the dark woods in the wind,
swaying, tree by tree.
You'll hardly ever find
more electrical fields.
Let us study the cloud mountains
from the Faraday cage.
When the lightning impresses,
we donate applause.
Hear how the clouds relax
to raindrops drumming on the roof,
as they release tension and
drops combine to form a stream.
See distant lines lawn outside.
Then the thunder
fades away quickly.
The charges are blown away
with lips and tongues.

## INKONTINENT VON KONTINENT ZU KONTINENT (für Meteorologen)

Die Wolken dort am Himmel sind gigantische Blasen
voll Wasserdampf vermischt mit Atmosphärengasen,
die in Bezug auf ihre eig'nen Körperflüssigkeiten
dort in den hohen Höhen feiste Pläne ausarbeiten:
Diese werden nämlich über uns bald ausgeschieden.
Wenn ich das so sehe, scheint es mir schon längst
entschieden.
Erst steigt der Dunst zum Himmel und dann – nur
wenig später –
hilft da auch kein Bitten mehr und kein Katheter, Peter.
Sie mehren sich und ballen sich und ziehen permanent
inkontinent von Kontinent zu Kontinent.

Sie schlürfen
Wasserdampf, entschließen sich zu fließen und
ergießen sich,
sie schlecken
Tröpfchen ganz nach innen und sie rinnen wie von Sinnen.
Wir dienen ihrem Zwecke, sei's auch ungern zugegeben,
unter dieser Wolkendecke als Bettpfanne mal eben.
Hast Du erst einmal anerkannt, dass das genau so ist,
dann fragst Du Dich nie mehr, warum man dazu sagt:
„es pisst".
Zudem sagt man nur „Sauwetter", vertraue mir da blind,
weil, wie man dabei sieht, die Wolken wirklich Säue sind.
Sie nässen Landzunge und Seezunge und ziehen permanent
inkontinent von Kontinent zu Kontinent,
inkontinent von Kontinent zu Kontinent.

## FROM CONTINENT TO CONTINENT IN AN
## INCONTINENT WAY (for meteorologists)


Gigantic bubbles are these clouds above us in the sky,
filled with atmospheric gases and with steam, that's why
sleeping in high altitudes, they need us as bedpans.
Regarding their own body fluids, they do develop plans.
These fluids, soon excreted, will then drench us
                down below.
Seeing that, I think it's been decided long ago.
First, the vapor rises to the sky, a million liters,
then begging, pleading will not help us, nor will
                those catheters.
They multiply and cluster and they travel day by day
from continent to continent in an incontinent way.


They slurp
steam, they flow and pour from Tripoli to Trinidad,
they lick
droplets all the way in and they trickle like they're mad.
We serve them, well, reluctant to admit it, fellowman,
under this cloud cover as I said – as a bedpan.
Once you have accepted this, though it may make
                you frown,
you'll never ask yourself why people say:
                „it's pissing down".
Don't go telling me that I'm an odd fair weather friend,
they'll drench Pikes Peak and sea pikes, carp and carpet
                in the end,
then headland, sole and badland and they migrate,
                hear me say,
from continent to continent in an incontinent way.


115

# NEO-PANGÄA

(für Geowissenschaftler)

Zwischen Sparta und Jakarta eine Weltenschicht
erschwindeln:
Wandelnd auf tektonischen Erdkrusten-Plattenschindeln
mixt die Welt sich gut mit Goa, Bali, Mauna Loa
und das Pentagon kommt mit dem Krakatau nach Muroroa.

Wir setzen Stalagmiten, Stalaktiten in den Vatikan
und diesen nach Pjöngjang und jenes nach Tadschikistan.
Ist wo zu viel Europa, hilft ein Schwung voll Südkorea
uns beim Plattendrift in Richtung Neo-Pangäa.

Ein bisschen Skagerrak und eine Prise Kattegat
wird ein Knaller in Kampala, Mali, Bali und Rabat,
zwischen Kongobecken und zentralindischem Rücken
wird den Fuß von Rios Zuckerhut der Kreml schmücken.

Hatsushima kommt zu Lima, Kansas City nach Haiti,
Kermanschah mit Genua und Sanaa zu New York City,
wir platzieren einen Teil von Texas in der Barentssee
und schieben Tora-Bora über'n Globus nach Tahiti-eh.

Misch du die Wadis Djedi und el-Hudi, Shangri-La
mit En Gedi, Filicudi, Wattenscheid und Korsika,
Timbuktu, Ouagadougou, Uppsala, Dschalalabad
weil es in Gießen strömt und Castrop zuviel Rauxel hat.

## NEO-PANGAEA

(for geoscientists)


Between Sparta and Jakarta, we'll obtain a world by fraud,
tectonic plates and crustal shingles, dancefloors
              for a thought,
we'll place Pentagon and Krakatau right close to Moruroa,
the world, it mixes well with Goa, Bali, Mauna Loa.

If there's too much Europe, take a big dose of Korea,
it will help us on the plate drift towards our Neo-Pangaea.
We'll place stalagmites and stalactites all over Vatican
and then we'll take it with Pyongyang right to Tajikistan.

A pinch of Skagerrak and then a bit of Kattegat:
a blast in Kampala and Mali, Bali and Rabat,
between Congo Basin and central Indian back,
the Kremlin and the Sugarloaf will get an overpack.

We mix the wadis Djedi and el-Hudi, Shangri-La
with Ein Gedi, Filicudi, Wattenscheid and Corsica,
if you're in Castrop Rauxel, remember if you had
a pinch of Ouagadougou, Uppsala, Jalalabad.

Hatsushima comes to Lima, Kansas City to Haiti,
Kermanshah with Genoa and Sana'a to New York City.
We'll place a part of Texas into Barents Sea
make Tora Bora Bora Bora's peak, if you agree.

# NEO-PANGÄA II

(für Geowissenschaftler)

Auf einem Felsen am Golf von Oman
sitzt mit stoischer Ruhe der Leguan Julian,
denn er erwartet tatsächlich vom Plattendrift,
dass er ihn mal zum iranischen Cousin schifft.
Dreist? Er und sein Cousin sind hierzu erkoren:
Sie werden für immer gleich wiedergeboren.
Wenn Julians Felsen ins Meer erodiert,
dann wird Felsen für Felsen von ihm ausprobiert,
bis er den findet, auf dem er bequem
ein Zeitalter dösen kann und noch zudem
die Aussicht nach drüben genießen kann.
Da sitzt der dann dösend und sieht sie sich an,
zählt dabei gelassen elf Meteorite,
neben ihm wachsen die Sedimentite,
und tritt Magma durch Schichten in epischer Breite,
dann tritt Julian eben ein wenig zur Seite.

## NEO-PANGAEA II
(for geoscientists)


This iguana called stoical Julian
sits on a rock in the Gulf of Oman.
He waits for the plate drift to help him to ride
to his Iranian cousin on the other side.
Uppity arrogance? No, no, never.
Both are reborn and reborn forever.
If his rock once erodes into the sea,
Julian tries rock by rock patiently
'til he finds one on which he can easily doze
for an era and enjoy the views that arose.
He then sits and dozes, enjoys the sights,
relaxedly counts fourteen meteorites,
watches sedimentary rocks beside him grow,
and when layers below him crack open so
that hot magma appears to light up the night,
then Julian takes a small step to the side.

# SAUGETIER

(für Biologen)

Es trägt diese famose Trockennasen-Symbiose,
diese beispiellos konfuse, furiose, grandiose
Phase der Synthese, so die seriöse These,
der Trockennasenaffen halbe Phylogenese.
Uns zwei Hominiden, die, was bringt da jedes Reden,
schnöde ausgeladen aus dem Bioladen „Garten Eden",
doch noch gern im Süden baden, uns ist es beschieden,
unsren Seelenfrieden hier im Liegen grad zu schmieden.

Wir sind gebeten als Primaten, es scheint effektiv geraten,
uns zu des Lebens Zeiten zu verknoten, zu verdrahten,
sieh nur unsre Vorfahr'n, unter Glas und in Vitrinen,
die der Paläontologen Leidenschaft nun dienen.
Wie die Ammoniten und vereinzelt Lobopoden
liegen wir versteinert einst im marmornen Fußboden,
sind wir zwei umschlungen dereinst hier so fossiliert,
hast hoffentlich Du mein Genom zuvor schon gut kartiert.

Ich verfall in Schluckatmung, höre, ich gestehe,
wenn ich diese ungetarnte Warntracht vor mir sehe,
als Teil der Hominidenfauna liegst und schmeckst Du mir,
und darum gilt: Ich Säugetier, ich sauge gern an Dir.
Wenn ich jetzt als Trockennasenaffe vor Dir stehe
mit zwei trocknen Nüstern, opponierbar meine Zehe,
denk ich: Du bist derart Bio, Baby, Wurzel-Blätter-Traum,
komm mit mir phylogenetisch auf des Stammes Baum.

# MAMMAL

(for biologists)


This splendid, basal, dry nasal symbiosis,
this unprecedented confused phase synthesis,
carries the phylogeny of dry-nosed primates as us
in a furious, grandiose way, so the reputable thesis.
It is granted to us to find peace here, we're lying,
the two hominids of us, what good is trying,
we're disdainfully disinvited from the health food store
called „Garden of Eden", let's stop waiting at the
                        front door.

Let's take a dip in the South, it seems effectively advised,
to merge ourselves during lifetime, now that you're
                        apprised.
See our ancestors, conserved in a degrading fashion,
under glass they serve paleontologist's passion.
Like the ammonites, lobopodia, and many more,
we'll be petrified embracedly in the marble floor,
we will be fossilized here one day obliviously,
hopefully you will have mapped my genome previously.

I get into pump breathing, here's my declaration,
whenever I see this uncloaked warning coloration,
I will taste the hominid fauna and you will taste me, too,
therefor applies: As a mammal, I will suck on you.
I stand before you as a dry-nosed primate and I will show
you both of my dry nostrils and an opposable toe,
I think: You're so organic, root-and-leaves-dream,
                        come with me,
let's climb up and down the phylogenetic fruit tree.


121

## STRAUCHELN IM BUSCHWERK
(für Biologen)

Lass uns den Klatschmohn mit Erdrauch beehren,
lass uns die Feigwurz das Donnerkraut lehren,
den Spargel gurgeln, den Rettich retten,
uns bei der Kirschenschonung in Beeten betten,
die Tigerlilien offen tragen
und im Fokus des Krokus Wurzeln schlagen.
Sink ins Gebüsch, mangoldige Kesse,
ich zeig Dir den Brunnen gleich bei der Kresse,
Beifuß, Liebstöckel, zur Knollenschule,
wo ich um die Gunst unter Ginster buhle,
vergiss nicht, beim Bücken den Hohlzahn zu fletschen,
lass Dich bei den Wicken an den Quetschenbaum
                    quetschen,
im Rettichdickicht, beim Maulwurfpalast,
falls Du Bock auf den Gärtner hast.

## IN THE BUSHES
(for biologists)


Let's honor the poppy with fumitory,
gargle asparagus, rate the radish's glory,
wear your lilies open and focus the crocus,
where lovage and mint are to find their root locus,
let's embed ourselves close to the devil's berries
in beds below sweet, wild and sour cherries,
eat a cherry, a berry blindfold and guess,
I'll show you the fountain besides the cress,
I tout for the grace with my white goosefeet,
sink into gorse bushes, golden silverbeet,
close to the mole palace, visit the nodule school,
bare saw-tooth oaks, bring the right garden tool,
squeeze all the peas near the tree on the hill
if you have a mood for the gardener still.

# IM MAULWURFSHÜGEL
(für Biologen)

Du Azorengimpel, du südlicher Pudu.
Ich Graufußtölpel-Tier, ich großer Kudu,
frag' Dich jetzt als einer der sprechenden Raben:
kann's Streifenhörnchen denn Bandwürmer haben?
Kann man die Kaulquappen wirklich entlarven?
Woran erkennt man, was Maulwürfe warfen?
Helfen Igelfischstacheln gegen die Brandung?
Und bellen die Flughunde bei jeder Landung?
Und etwas hätte mich auch interessiert:
Bleibt ein Stachelschwein Stachelschwein,
                    wenn man's rasiert?
Verträgt man als Pustelschwein die Pubertät?
Ich maulender Maulwurf, der hier vor Dir steht,
hab mir, so scheint es, Dich zugezogen.
Ich habe nun dieses und jenes erwogen.
Doch es scheint mir bestimmt, wildbiologisch,
ich bin darauf festgelegt, ganz zoologisch:
also zügel' die Flügel, bis ich sie Dir bügel'
und komm mit mir in meinen Maulwurfshügel.

## INSIDE THE MOLE HILL
(for biologists)


You Azores bullfinch, you southerly pudu.
me, Abbott's booby, me, the large kudu,
as a small talking raven, I ask you in plain terms:
can all these rope squirrels really have tapeworms?
What if a small mole is born with a big mole?
Are there any tadpoles close to the North Pole?
Is bloodsuckers gut ache caused by too much scurf?
Can porcupine fish spines help surfers to surf?
I ask you as one of the small talking raven:
Is a porky a porky still once it is shaven?
As a warthog, how does teenage puberty feel?
Me, mound forming mole, caught by your appeal,
I brought you upon myself, that's how it seems.
I have now considered some things in my dreams.
To me, it's determined, it's fixed biologically,
this defines you and me quite zoologically:
Using your wings is wrong, I have two bowls, still,
come with me now, deep into my molehill.

## ZUNDERSCHWAMM
(für Biologen)

Wenn ich beim Schleimigen Schüppling dich wähne,
dann keimt eine Kopfige Gallertträne
beim Fleischgrauen Knorpelporling, der heuchelnd
mit Schimmel Lorcheln und Morcheln meuchelt.
Dieser geistige Risspilz ist knollenlos.
Ich erschnüffel die Trüffel beim Drehzahnmoos.
Unter dem Blattdach zur Pilzbalz im Moosfilz,
im Unterholz als Kiefernfilzporlings-Moorpilz,
wo Spindelsporige Fälblinge modern,
werd als Beringter Flämmling ich lodern
für dich, Hexenröhrlingin, psychoaktiv,
neben der auf dem Moos eine Nonne nackt schlief,
gegen Dich sind so Fruchtkörper Krause Glucken,
die sich vor Herkuleskeulen wegducken,
denn du, mein Gezonter Ohrlappenpilz,
sporst immer am Rande des Overkills.

126

## TINDER FUNGUS
(for biologists)


If I suspect you besides the red raspberry slime,
I feel like a weeping bolete still at times.
He who murders the morels belongs into jail,
he's a mud-born stinkhorn and a false turkey tail,
he is a smut fungus cause his slippery jack
is a dead man's finger, so don't you look back,
I am the artist's conk, the lion's mane mushroom,
I will leave your velvet shanks red, in a lush bloom,
under the sheet roof of morel's mating site.
I will nuzzle the truffles where hornworts hide.
Where radiating phlebias decay,
in the undergrowth as silky parchments we'll lay.
I'll blaze as an earthstar for you, but above all,
I am the comb tooth, my gem-studded puffball.
When I see you, soft slipper, scarletina bolete,
I know no hen of the woods could ever compete,
against you, other fruiting bodies are cramp balls,
banned to where the earth-boring dung beetle still crawls,
my dryad's saddle, my elegant polypore,
on the brink of mere overkill you will spore.

## AN DEN SCHAMANEN MIT KREIDETABLETTE
(für Mediziner)

Sein ganzes ZNS
schlägt Blasen bis zur Stirn.
Hilft da eine hochgelobte,
hochmoderne Heilbehandlung?
Im Rückenmark sein Es
schafft Blutarmut im Hirn.
Hilft da nur die alterprobte
Hacke-Hackebeilbehandlung?

Sie städtischer Schamane
mit Kreidekautablette.
Was ist jetzt der Schlüssel?
Was bringt die Pharmazie?
Da ist jener Kumpane,
den ich gern weiter hätte.
Heilt Sprünge in der Schüssel
die Gefäße-Chirurgie?

Lässt sich in Quarantäne packen!
Frisst aus ihrer Hand den Käse!
Er war sonst gegen jede
Erregerin immun.
Lässt sich auf ihre Lehne sacken!
Anamnese: Hirnprothese?
Doc, was steht in Rede?
Was kann man nun tun?

## TO THE SHAMAN WITH THE CHALK PILL
(for medics)


His entire CNS
blisters like his brain.
I'm puzzled, I admit.
I'm looking for your help.
Will only, as I guess,
a cleaver heal the pain?
In his spinal cord the id
turns his brain to kelp.

There's this friendly dude,
I once called him a friend.
She cans him just like a sardine!
What can I do, what is the key
to heal the brain she barbecued?
Eats cream cheese from her hand!
She puts him in quarantine!
What's the advice of pharmacy?

Sags down on her backrest!
Would a brain prosthesis
help, what is at issue, doc?
What can we do, what helps us now?
You urban shaman, say, at best,
what's the anamnesis?
Take your chalk pills and your smock
and help to free this dork somehow.

## FRAGEN EINER VERÄNGSTIGTEN ÖFFENTLICH-KEIT ZUR SEUCHENGEFAHR
(für Mediziner)

Würden wir weiter Palaver inszenieren,
während Viren in Kadavern jubilieren?
Würden wegen der grassierenden Viren
vagabundierende Wandernieren kollidieren?
Würden wir Viren mitkopieren, wenn in Kopierpapieren
Viren wären?
Würde man uns das auf die Kanaren fahren verwehren?
Würden Virenabwehrer ihre Würde bewahren?
Würde Prämiensparen weiterhin Bewährung erfahren?
Würden Viren gären in allen Abflussrohren,
wären all unsere Poren voller Virensporen?
Würden die, denen Torturen widerfuhren,
nicht mehr vor Virenprofiteuren spuren
und Kämpfe mit verchlorten Rohren aufführen,
während Terroristen uns Anti-Antiviren unterrühren?
Gäbe es, weil Virenforscher Viren frisieren, Virenfrisuren?
Wären die Haare solcher Virenfriseure voller Virenspuren?
Wüssten wir, welche die wahren Viren wären?
Würden sich auch an Hurenohrenhaaren Viren mehren?

## QUESTIONS OF A TERRIFIED PUBLIC ABOUT DISEASE RISKS
(for medics)


Will viruses in cadavers rejoice
if we continue to stage palaver furthermore?
Would stray floating kidneys collide
because there are rampant viruses galore?
Would virus defenders maintain their dignity?
Would they deny us the ferry to the Canaries?
Would all our pores be full of virus spores?
Will Mira still score in her airy pinafores?
Would we no longer obey virus profiteers?
Would insurances continue to help against fears?
Did terrorists stir us anti-antiviruses before?
Would virus researchers prepare for far more?
Would some of their varied viruses have hair?
Regular hairdressers, will they still care?
Would viruses ferment in all drain pipes fairly
to ensnare carnivores and herbivores unawarely?
How would we know where the true viruses were?
Will viruses multiply on whore's ear hair?

# WIR SIND H2O
## (für Chemiker)

| $H_2O$ | $H_2O$ | $H_2O$ | $H_2O$ | $H_2O$ | $H_2O$ | $H_2O$ | $H_2O$ | $H_2O$ | $H_2O$ | $H_2O$ | $H_2O$ | $H_2O$ | $H_2O$ | $H_2O$ | $H_2O$ |
|---|---|---|---|---|---|---|---|---|---|---|---|---|---|---|---|
| $H_2O$ | 23 | 68 | 16 | 63 | 6 | 1 | 62 | $H_2O$ | 5 | 33 | 53 | 16 | $H_2O$ | $H_2O$ | $H_2O$ |
| $H_2O$ | V | Er | S | Eu | C | H | Te | $H_2O$ | B | As | I | S | $H_2O$ | $H_2O$ | $H_2O$ |
| $H_2O$ | $H_2O$ | $H_2O$ | $H_2O$ | $H_2O$ | $H_2O$ | $H_2O$ | $H_2O$ | $H_2O$ | $H_2O$ | $H_2O$ | $H_2O$ | $H_2O$ | $H_2O$ | $H_2O$ | $H_2O$ |
| $H_2O$ | 15 | 57 | 16 | 22 | 19 | 4 | 111 | $H_2O$ | 49 | $H_2O$ | 74 | 33 | 16 | 68 | $H_2O$ |
| $H_2O$ | P | La | S | Tl | K | Be | Rg | $H_2O$ | In | $H_2O$ | W | As | S | Er | $H_2O$ |
| $H_2O$ | $H_2O$ | $H_2O$ | $H_2O$ | $H_2O$ | $H_2O$ | $H_2O$ | $H_2O$ | $H_2O$ | $H_2O$ | $H_2O$ | $H_2O$ | $H_2O$ | $H_2O$ | $H_2O$ | $H_2O$ |
| $H_2O$ | 19 | 92 | 99 | 62 | 7 | 4 | 74 | 53 | 1 | 7 | 68 | $H_2O$ | $H_2O$ | $H_2O$ | $H_2O$ |
| $H_2O$ | K | U | Es | Te | N | Be | W | O | H | N | Er | $H_2O$ | $H_2O$ | $H_2O$ | $H_2O$ |
| $H_2O$ | $H_2O$ | $H_2O$ | $H_2O$ | $H_2O$ | $H_2O$ | $H_2O$ | $H_2O$ | $H_2O$ | $H_2O$ | $H_2O$ | $H_2O$ | $H_2O$ | $H_2O$ | $H_2O$ | $H_2O$ |
| $H_2O$ | $H_2O$ | 23 | 68 | 0 | 6 | 19 | $H_2O$ | 53 | 1 | 102 | $H_2O$ | 72 | 109 | 95 | $H_2O$ |
| $H_2O$ | $H_2O$ | V | Er | Re | C | K | $H_2O$ | O | H | Ne | $H_2O$ | Ta | Mt | Am | $H_2O$ |
| $H_2O$ | $H_2O$ | $H_2O$ | $H_2O$ | $H_2O$ | $H_2O$ | $H_2O$ | $H_2O$ | $H_2O$ | $H_2O$ | $H_2O$ | $H_2O$ | $H_2O$ | $H_2O$ | $H_2O$ | $H_2O$ |
| $H_2O$ | $H_2O$ | $H_2O$ | $H_2O$ | $H_2O$ | $H_2O$ | $H_2O$ | $H_2O$ | 53 | 1 | 102 | $H_2O$ | 19 | 57 | 32 | $H_2O$ |
| $H_2O$ | $H_2O$ | $H_2O$ | $H_2O$ | $H_2O$ | $H_2O$ | $H_2O$ | $H_2O$ | O | H | Ne | $H_2O$ | K | La | Ge | $H_2O$ |
| $H_2O$ | $H_2O$ | $H_2O$ | $H_2O$ | $H_2O$ | $H_2O$ | $H_2O$ | $H_2O$ | $H_2O$ | $H_2O$ | $H_2O$ | $H_2O$ | $H_2O$ | $H_2O$ | $H_2O$ | $H_2O$ |
| $H_2O$ | 6 | 53 | *2* | $H_2O$ | 9 | 92 | 68 | $H_2O$ | 114 | 53 | 88 | $H_2O$ | $H_2O$ | $H_2O$ | $H_2O$ |
| $H_2O$ | C | O | | $H_2O$ | F | U | Er | $H_2O$ | Fl | O | Ra | $H_2O$ | $H_2O$ | $H_2O$ | $H_2O$ |
| $H_2O$ | $H_2O$ | $H_2O$ | $H_2O$ | $H_2O$ | $H_2O$ | $H_2O$ | $H_2O$ | $H_2O$ | $H_2O$ | $H_2O$ | $H_2O$ | $H_2O$ | $H_2O$ | $H_2O$ | $H_2O$ |
| $H_2O$ | $H_2O$ | $H_2O$ | $H_2O$ | $H_2O$ | $H_2O$ | $H_2O$ | $H_2O$ | 92 | 60 | $H_2O$ | 32 | 74 | 68 | 4 | $H_2O$ |
| $H_2O$ | $H_2O$ | $H_2O$ | $H_2O$ | $H_2O$ | $H_2O$ | $H_2O$ | $H_2O$ | U | Nd | $H_2O$ | Ge | W | Er | Be | $H_2O$ |
| $H_2O$ | $H_2O$ | $H_2O$ | $H_2O$ | $H_2O$ | $H_2O$ | $H_2O$ | $H_2O$ | $H_2O$ | $H_2O$ | $H_2O$ | $H_2O$ | $H_2O$ | $H_2O$ | $H_2O$ | $H_2O$ |
| $H_2O$ | 16 | 53 | $H_2O$ | 16 | 47 | 7 | $H_2O$ | 23 | 68 | 16 | 63 | 6 | 1 | 62 | $H_2O$ |
| $H_2O$ | S | O | $H_2O$ | S | Ag | N | $H_2O$ | V | Er | S | Eu | C | H | Te | $H_2O$ |
| $H_2O$ | $H_2O$ | $H_2O$ | $H_2O$ | $H_2O$ | $H_2O$ | $H_2O$ | $H_2O$ | $H_2O$ | $H_2O$ | $H_2O$ | $H_2O$ | $H_2O$ | $H_2O$ | $H_2O$ | $H_2O$ |
| $H_2O$ | $H_2O$ | $H_2O$ | $H_2O$ | $H_2O$ | $H_2O$ | $H_2O$ | 11 | 22 | 53 | 11 | 2 | 16 | 62 | 7 | $H_2O$ |
| $H_2O$ | $H_2O$ | $H_2O$ | $H_2O$ | $H_2O$ | $H_2O$ | $H_2O$ | Na | Ti | O | Na | Li | S | Te | N | $H_2O$ |
| $H_2O$ | $H_2O$ | $H_2O$ | $H_2O$ | $H_2O$ | $H_2O$ | $H_2O$ | $H_2O$ | $H_2O$ | $H_2O$ | $H_2O$ | $H_2O$ | $H_2O$ | $H_2O$ | $H_2O$ | $H_2O$ |
| $H_2O$ | 74 | 77 | $H_2O$ | 14 | 60 | $H_2O$ | 1 | *2* | 53 | $H_2O$ | $H_2O$ | $H_2O$ | $H_2O$ | $H_2O$ | $H_2O$ |
| $H_2O$ | W | Ir | $H_2O$ | Si | Nd | $H_2O$ | H | | O | $H_2O$ | $H_2O$ | $H_2O$ | $H_2O$ | $H_2O$ | $H_2O$ |
| $H_2O$ | $H_2O$ | $H_2O$ | $H_2O$ | $H_2O$ | $H_2O$ | $H_2O$ | $H_2O$ | $H_2O$ | $H_2O$ | $H_2O$ | $H_2O$ | $H_2O$ | $H_2O$ | $H_2O$ | $H_2O$ |
| $H_2O$ | 53 | 1 | 102 | $H_2O$ | 13 | 53 | 83 | $H_2O$ | $H_2O$ | $H_2O$ | $H_2O$ | $H_2O$ | 74 | 77 | $H_2O$ |
| $H_2O$ | O | H | Ne | $H_2O$ | Al | I | Bi | $H_2O$ | $H_2O$ | $H_2O$ | $H_2O$ | $H_2O$ | W | Ir | $H_2O$ |
| $H_2O$ | $H_2O$ | $H_2O$ | $H_2O$ | $H_2O$ | $H_2O$ | $H_2O$ | $H_2O$ | $H_2O$ | $H_2O$ | $H_2O$ | $H_2O$ | $H_2O$ | $H_2O$ | $H_2O$ | $H_2O$ |
| $H_2O$ | 6 | 92 | 6 | 2 | 7 | $H_2O$ | 74 | 77 | $H_2O$ | 1 | 53 | 9 | 26 | 7 | $H_2O$ |
| $H_2O$ | S | U | C | He | N | $H_2O$ | W | Ir | $H_2O$ | H | O | F | Fe | N | $H_2O$ |
| $H_2O$ | $H_2O$ | $H_2O$ | $H_2O$ | $H_2O$ | $H_2O$ | $H_2O$ | $H_2O$ | $H_2O$ | $H_2O$ | $H_2O$ | $H_2O$ | $H_2O$ | $H_2O$ | $H_2O$ | $H_2O$ |

# I AM H2O

## (for chemists)

|  |  |  |  |  |  |  |  |  |  |  |  |  |  |  |  |
|---|---|---|---|---|---|---|---|---|---|---|---|---|---|---|---|
| H₂O | H₂O | H₂O | H₂O | H₂O | H₂O | H₂O | H₂O | H₂O | H₂O | H₂O | H₂O | H₂O | H₂O | H₂O | H₂O |
| H₂O | 90 Th | 53 I | 16 S | H₂O | 16 S | 8 O | 71 Lu | 22 Ti | 8 O | 7 N | H₂O | H₂O | H₂O | H₂O | H₂O |
| H₂O | H₂O | H₂O | H₂O | H₂O | H₂O | H₂O | H₂O | H₂O | H₂O | H₂O | H₂O | H₂O | H₂O | H₂O | H₂O |
| H₂O | H₂O | H₂O | H₂O | H₂O | H₂O | 53 I | 16 S | H₂O | 16 S | 53 I | 6 C | 19 K | H₂O | H₂O | H₂O |
| H₂O | H₂O | H₂O | H₂O | H₂O | H₂O | H₂O | H₂O | H₂O | H₂O | H₂O | H₂O | H₂O | H₂O | H₂O | H₂O |
| H₂O | 53 I | 58 Ce | 4 Be | 111 Rg | 16 S | H₂O | 8 O | 9 F | H₂O | 15 P | 57 La | 16 S | 22 Ti | 6 C | H₂O |
| H₂O | H₂O | H₂O | H₂O | H₂O | H₂O | H₂O | H₂O | H₂O | H₂O | H₂O | H₂O | H₂O | H₂O | H₂O | H₂O |
| H₂O | 53 I | 16 S | 57 La | 60 Nd | 16 S | H₂O | 92 U | 60 Nd | 68 Er | H₂O | H₂O | H₂O | H₂O | H₂O | H₂O |
| H₂O | H₂O | H₂O | H₂O | H₂O | H₂O | H₂O | H₂O | H₂O | H₂O | H₂O | H₂O | H₂O | H₂O | H₂O | H₂O |
| H₂O | H₂O | H₂O | H₂O | H₂O | H₂O | 74 W | 85 At | 68 Er | H₂O | 84 Po | 53 I | 16 S | 8 O | 60 Nd | H₂O |
| H₂O | H₂O | H₂O | H₂O | H₂O | H₂O | H₂O | H₂O | H₂O | H₂O | H₂O | H₂O | H₂O | H₂O | H₂O | H₂O |
| H₂O | 5 B | 33 As | 53 I | 16 S | H₂O | 8 O | 9 F | H₂O | 3 Li | 26 Fe | H₂O | H₂O | H₂O | H₂O | H₂O |
| H₂O | H₂O | H₂O | H₂O | H₂O | H₂O | H₂O | H₂O | H₂O | H₂O | H₂O | H₂O | H₂O | H₂O | H₂O | H₂O |
| H₂O | H₂O | H₂O | H₂O | H₂O | H₂O | H₂O | H₂O | H₂O | H₂O | 102 No | H₂O | 13 Al | 53 I | 83 Bi | H₂O |
| H₂O | H₂O | H₂O | H₂O | H₂O | H₂O | H₂O | H₂O | H₂O | H₂O | H₂O | H₂O | H₂O | H₂O | H₂O | H₂O |
| H₂O | 92 U | H₂O | 18 Ar | H₂O | 1 H | 2 | 53 O | H₂O | 4 Be | 20 Ca | 92 U | 34 Se | H₂O | H₂O | H₂O |
| H₂O | H₂O | H₂O | H₂O | H₂O | H₂O | H₂O | H₂O | H₂O | H₂O | H₂O | H₂O | H₂O | H₂O | H₂O | H₂O |
| H₂O | H₂O | H₂O | H₂O | H₂O | 53 I | H₂O | 95 Am | H₂O | 1 H | 2 | 53 O | H₂O | H₂O | H₂O | H₂O |
| H₂O | H₂O | H₂O | H₂O | H₂O | H₂O | H₂O | H₂O | H₂O | H₂O | H₂O | H₂O | H₂O | H₂O | H₂O | H₂O |
| H₂O | 67 Ho | 15 P | 68 Er | 16 S | H₂O | H₂O | H₂O | 53 I | 7 N | H₂O | 34 Se | 18 Ar | 6 C | 1 H | H₂O |
| H₂O | H₂O | H₂O | H₂O | H₂O | H₂O | H₂O | H₂O | H₂O | H₂O | H₂O | H₂O | H₂O | H₂O | H₂O | H₂O |
| H₂O | H₂O | H₂O | H₂O | H₂O | 8 O | 9 F | H₂O | 16 S | 8 O | 71 Lu | 22 Ti | 8 O | 7 N | 16 S | H₂O |
| H₂O | H₂O | H₂O | H₂O | H₂O | H₂O | H₂O | H₂O | H₂O | H₂O | H₂O | H₂O | H₂O | H₂O | H₂O | H₂O |

previously published in: the Offbeat, Volume 17, 2016

## DOOFNICKEL

(für Chemiker)

(zwei bayrische Chemiker streiten sich um die einzige
Dame im Labor)


B: „He, Ti Li Na, Ti Li Na, Ti Li Na, O, O.“
C: „Ar Ti Li Na Mg Si Ni, Na, Si Ni, O No.“
B: „Am Ar, Si Nickel, I Mo Ag Ti Li Na,
Ti Li Na S Mo In, Si Kobalt, Ca P I Ta?“
C: „Scandium H Au N, I Mg Ti Li Na, Ta Ta!
Vanadium H Au Th, I Bor Si, H H!“

**Glasaugenstern** – 101 Gedichte von Alex Dreppec
Mit Illustrationen von Nicola Koch, Axel Röthemeyer, Eva Simone
Scheuermann, Alex Dreppec, chiliverlag 2014
ISBN 978-3-943292-21-3, 156 Seiten, EURO 8,90

In dieser Sammlung stehen zuvor an über hundert Orten verstreut
abgedruckte Gedichte erstmals nebeneinander und geben einen
vielfältigen Einblick in das bunte Schaffen eines der führenden komi-
schen Lyriker der Gegenwart.

Alex Dreppec war 2002 Finalist der deutschsprachigen Poetry Slam-
Meisterschaften in Bern. 2004 wurde er mit dem Wilhelm-Busch-Preis
ausgezeichnet. Dreppec veröffentlichte Lyrik, Essays und Kurzprosa
in zahlreichen Anthologien (u.a. 2008 in „Der Große Conrady" und in
„Parody on Impression", New York).

# OHNE GLEICHUNG

## (für Mathematiker)

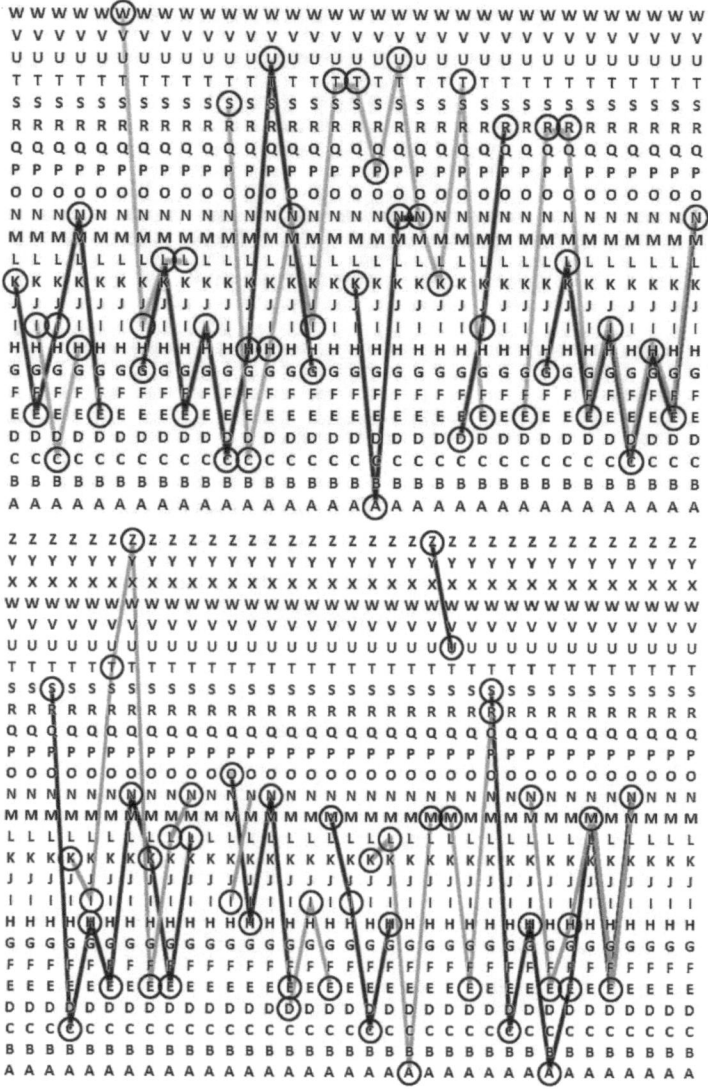

# WITHOUT EQUATION
## (for mathematicians)

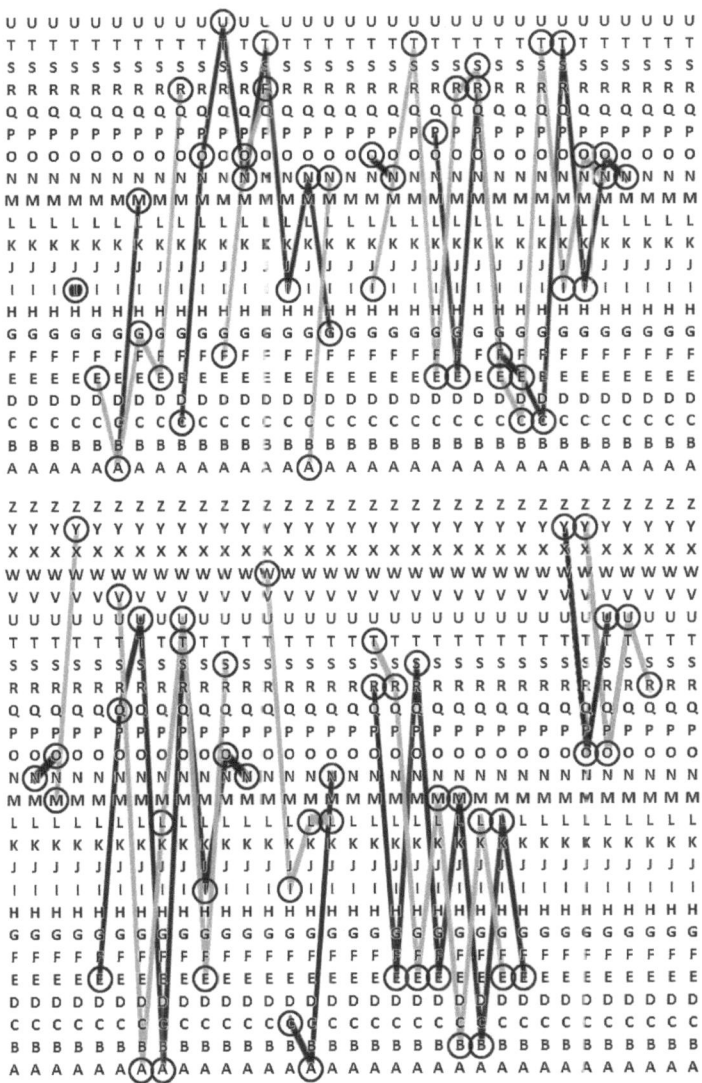

pto

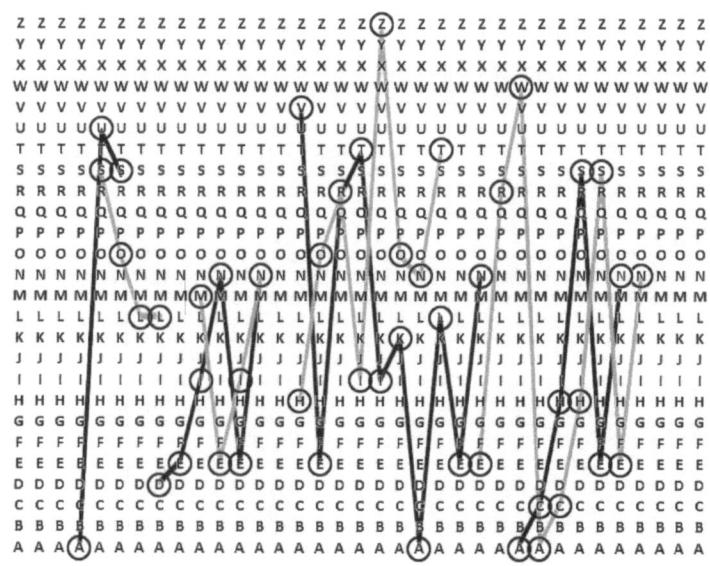

## OHNE GLEICHUNG
### (für Mathematiker)

Keine Gleichung kann Dir gleichen
Ich will Schnittpunkte erreichen
Schenkel ohne mich zu schämen
kitzeln in die Klammer nehmen
Aus deinen vertikalen Achsen
soll mein Horizont erwachsen

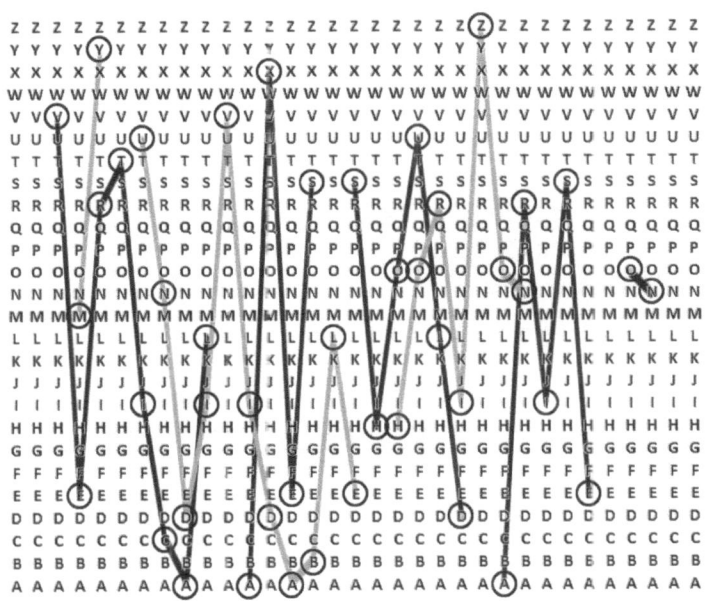

## WITHOUT EQUATION
### (for mathematicians)

I am counting on perfection
eager for an intersection
no equation can resemble you
my values will tremble your
vertical axes should arise on
my undividable horizon

## ATOMAROMA

(für Chemiker)

Meines so wie deines Körpers schwere Elemente,
Teile eminenter kosmischer Experimente,
sind dereinst in Supernova-Blitzlichtern entstanden,
wo entkernte Kerne sich zu Kernen gern verbanden,
Elektronen reagieren in Laboridyllen,
enthüllen im Substanz-Tanz ihrer prallen Hüllen Füllen –
und Finger rein und abgeleckt,
Atom-Aromen abgecheckt,
mit LSD zum PSE,
mit schwerem 2H und hohem C.

Im Bauch von Reagenz-Glaskolben findet sich's zusammen:
Dampf und Rauch und Knall und Gold und blaue Flammen,
vollere Spektrallinien in grellen Prismen,
schon von Alchemisten viel gesuchte Mechanismen,
bis Kohlenstoff zur Kurzweil in der Säure Ketten knüpft,
dir deine Base angesäuert in die Beize hüpft –
und Finger rein und abgeleckt,
Atom-Aromen abgecheckt,
mit LSD zum PSE,
mit schwerem 2H und hohem C.

## ATOM AROMA

(for chemists)


Your body's, my body's heavier elements
took part in eminent cosmic experiments,
born once in big supernova's space flashes,
where nuclei formed out of nuclei's ashes.
Now electrons will do their substance dance well,
shelling the fullness of their shrillest shell,
this atom flavor, pick it up,
put your finger in and lick it up,
the periodic table and LSD,
then heavy 2H and a high C.

Steam, smoke and blue flames, 'cos this is the task,
are caught in the realm of a reagent flask,
prisms, they fill with light, split up in spectral lines,
until the alchemist's brooding mind really shines.
Carbon links chains and chains pastime to pastime,
this base will hop in the stain for the last time.
This atom flavor, pick it up,
put your finger in and lick it up,
the periodic table and LSD,
then heavy-2H and a high C.

## PULSAR IM SCHÄDEL

(für Physiker)

Du kommst auch nicht gänzlich ungekrümmt herum
um dieser Dimension Raum-Zeit-Kontinuum,
sie denkt in Hyperdimensionen, er denkt in Superpositionen,
auf sie warten die Protonen, für sie sausen Elektronen.
Du siehst im Prisma prima jede Plasmaspur
und schaust ins schwarze Loch von Mütterchen Natur,
der Jet dieses Neutronensterns ist Gottes Fliegenpatsche
und zack ist der Pulsar direkt an deiner Klatsche.

Hast du Leptonen, ach, und auch Hadronen, ach,
studiert sowie die Wechselwirkung, stark und schwach,
stehende Welle wohl gewägt und Lissajous-Figuren,
amorphes Mat'rial gegen Kristallstrukturen,
weißt doch, dass dein Leib selbst auch nur ein Teilchen ist
mit Heisenbergscher Unschärfe, wenn man ihn misst.
Legt so gekrümmte Raum-Zeit auch mal Falten
                auf die Stirn:
bald pulsiert dir ein Pulsar direkt im Physikerhirn.

# PULSAR IN THE SKULL
(for physicists)


Your brain will not get out of this unbruised,
      my nosy friend,
this space-time curvature will also bend you in the end:
They think in high positions, they think in high dimensions,
they'll shock the protons of your brain with
      electronic tensions.
Within the prism, plasma traces shine, a gloriole,
you'll take a look deep into Mother Nature's big black hole.
God's fly flaps: jets of neutron stars. A crackle in the phone.
There's a pulsar deep inside of science's cranial bone.

Is your body just a particle itself, in pain and pleasure,
with Heisenberg's uncertainty not only when it's measured?
Study leptons, hadrons, interactions, strong and weak,
standing waves before your eyes are taken to the peak,
this space-time curvature inside the brain accumulates,
causes wrinkles on the forehead: a physicist pulsates,
watches supernovas spit out heavy gallstones and brimstone.
There's a pulsar deep inside this science's cranial bone.

# EXOPLANETIN
## (für Physiker)

Nach der Radialgeschwindigkeitsmethode.
Ich analysierte deine Atmosphäre *(wer pflügt deine Äcker?)*
beim Transit vor einem anderen Stern *(du entfixt*
*deine eiernde Mutter)*,
dessen Licht dadurch einknickte.
Als es deine Lufthülle durchdrang,
schicktest du dunkle Linien in meine Richtung.

Deine Volumenprozente:
77,6 % N2,        21,3 % O2,

Spurengase:
CO2 0,1 %        CH4,

Nahezu außerirdisch.

Nun weiß ich: du bist in der habitablen Zone.
Da ist eine Biosphäre *(wer pflügt deine Äcker?)*
und ich *(du entfixt deine eiernde Mutter)* werde
sie nie sehen.

## EXOPLANETRESS

(for physicists)

By the radial velocity method.
I analyzed your atmosphere *(who plows your fields?)*
while you were transiting another star *(you dislocate your*
*wobbling mother)*
whose light therefore dimmed.
When it penetrated your atmosphere,
you were sending dark lines in my direction.

Your percentages by volume:
0,5 % Ar,      0,3 % Kr.

Trace gasses:
O3,      SO2.

Almost extraterrestrial.

Now I know: you are within the habitable zone.
There is a biosphere *(who plows your fields?)*
and I *(you displace your wobbling mother)* will never
get to see it.

previously published in: „Before Passing", Great Weather for Media, 2015

## GEQUANTELTE MATERIE
(für Physiker)

Warte, warte nur ein Weilchen,
dann sind wir verschränkte Teilchen.
Gegen den Uhrzeigersinn – spinn ich
spukhaft ist das. Wahrhaft übersinnlich.
Unser undefinierter Spin spinnt nie.
Denn im Uhrzeigersinn, sieh nur hin, spinnt sie.


## KEIN RECHENFEHLER
(für Mathematiker)

Bei der Vermehrung gilt oft: „Gott freut sich ungrader
Zahlen." (Vergil, Eklogen VIII, 75)
Da macht eins plus eins dann drei, mit Kinderhand
zu malen.
So kommt nach mancher Kurvendiskussionen Enge
ein Pünktchen mehr hinein in eine kleinste Menge
und berührt die Summen aller Nenner, aller Zähler.
Nur nach Knaus Ogino wohl ein Rechenfehler.

## QUANTIZED MATTER
(for physicists)


Wait just a while until you and me
are entangled particles, you'll see.
Counterclockwise – I will spin
my net around you, spooky like a djin.
Our undefined spin never falters, you'll see,
for clockwise, you'll spin your net around me.


## NOT A MISCALCULATION
(for mathematicians)


„God delights in odd numbers" is true for propagation, too.
One plus one makes three, write it in pink and baby blue.
So, at the end of some narrow curve sketching, let us bet,
one more speck appears within a smallest set
and affects the total of all counter's dear denomination.
After Knaus Ogino, that's a miscalculation.

# WAHRSCHEINLICHKEITSRECHNUNG
## (für Mathematiker)

Du kannst im wahren Wirrwarr der Wahrscheinlichkeiten,
in n-dimensionalen Mannigfaltigkeiten
chaostheoretischen Fraktalen, Hilberträumen
begegnen in athletisch-arithmetischen Träumen,
mit Abu'l Wafa über weite Wüstenwege gleiten,
mit Al-Battani über alhazensche Dünen reiten,
dann mit Aryabhata über Arabiens Zahlen walten,
in Oasen der Erkenntnis Zahlenwelten gestalten.
Du kannst überall und jederzeit mit Zahlen rechnen,
und dabei auch mit Künstler-Glück und Künstler-Pech,
denn:
nach der Unendlichkeit unendlichen Paradoxien
wird Dich schlicht ein Magenknurren auf die Erde ziehen.

## PROBABILITY CALCULATION
(for mathematicians)


Within the great tangle of probabilities,
within n-dimensional manifolds,
chaos theoretical fractals, you can meet
Hilbert spaces in athletic-arithmetic dreams,
hover with Abu'l Wafa over long desert ways,
ride with Al-Battani on Alhazen's dunes,
then brood with Aryabhata over Arabic figures,
you can customize the number worlds of knowledge
in oases.
You have to expect numbers anywhere, anytime,
and thereby also good luck and hard luck because:
after infinity's endless paradoxes,
a growl of the stomach will pull you back to earth.

# SCHÜLER ZUR MA THEMATIK
(für Mathematiker)

Ma Thematik
Ma Thema tik
Ma Thema tik tick
Ma Thema Taktik
Ma Thema hip
Ma Thema Hip Hop
Ma Thema schick

Mathema Schock
Mathema tock
Mathema tock tock
Mathema Zick Zack
Mathema Schnick Schnack
Ma Thema Abfuck
Mathema rate ma kack

## PUPILS ABOUT MATHEMATICS
(for mathematicians)


Ma thematic s
Ma theme a tick
Ma theme a tick tick
Ma theme a tactics
Ma theme a hip
Ma theme a hip hop
Ma theme a chic

Mathema shock
Mathema toc
Mathema tick tock
Mathema zig zag
Mathema knick knack
Ma theme a fuck
Ma theme guess what shit

## WAS WIRKLICH ZÄHLT
### (für Mathematiker)

Darf ich an Variablen drehn?
Darf ich dir auf den Zähler gehn?
Am Wendepunkt der Division
biet' ich dir Hochzahl, Stammfunktion,
die sich da im Dreieck häuft,
wo's gleichschenklig zusammenläuft.
Betrieb ich doch so lange schon
am Horizont der Achse
dieser Kurven Diskussion,
auf dass die Steigung wachse.

Um 180 Grad gedreht,
sei Du. Wie dann der Vektor steht?
Wenn mir jetzt kein Skalarprodukt
noch bei Dir in die Suppe spuckt,
wir die Macht der Dividenden
zwischen uns beenden,
summieren wir uns auf und dann,
ins Unendliche gespiegelt,
nimmt's positive Werte an.
Dein Schicksal ist besiegelt.

## WHAT REALLY COUNTS
(for mathematicians)


May I spin your variables now?
May I get up on your counter somehow?
The time is right for more precision
here at the end of the division.
Root function, triangle, exponent,
all foster one more component
that runs together, we will see,
for you and me isoscelesly.
On the horizon of the axis,
your curve sketching now backs us.

You're rotated by X degrees,
where's the vector situated, please?
Now that it seems that no scalar
has been spotted in my soup so far,
the dividends between us
are deleted from my screen, thus,
we add up to ourselves and then,
we're mirrored infinitely when
your fate is sealed, it's causative,
the values all get positive.

# 4

# Technik / Engineering

## CHECKLISTE: ANFORDERUNGEN AN TECHNISCHE GEDICHTE (Ausschnitt) / CHECKLIST: REQUIREMENTS OF TECHNICAL POEMS (excerpt)

(für Maschinenbauer /
for mechanical engineers)


1. Technisch-wirtschaftliche Anforderungen / Technical and economic requirements

1.1. Technische Anforderungen / Technical requirements
Schwingungen? Statik der Zeilen? / Vibrations? Statics of the lines?
Gebrauchsdauer? / Service life?
Verschleiß der Metaphern? / Wear of metaphors?
Korrosion? (...) / Corrosion? (...)

1.2. Schnittstellen / Interfaces
1.2.1 Technische Umgebung / Technical environment
Wartung und Instandhaltung? / Service and maintenance?
1.2.2 Mensch, Gesellschaft, Umwelt: / People, society, environment:
Energiebedarf (Autor, Verlag, Druckerei, Leser)? / Energy supplies (author, publisher, printers, reader)?
Emissionen (Papier, Druckfarbe, Metaphern)? / Emissions (paper, ink, metaphors)?
Sicherheit (Ablenkung von Umweltgefahren)? / Safety (distraction from environmental hazards)?
Recycling?

1.3. Kosten des Gedichts / Cost of the poem
Fertigungs-/Montagekosten? / Manufacturing/assembly costs?

Logistikkosten? / Logistics costs?
Inbetriebnahmekosten? / Startup costs?
Betriebs-/Instandhaltungskosten? / Operating, maintenance costs?
Entsorgungskosten? / Disposal costs?

1.4. Gesetze, Normen, Garantien / Laws, standards, guarantees
Schutzrechte? / Trade mark rights?
Unfallverhütungsvorschriften (UVV)? / Occupational health and safety standards
TÜV-Vorschriften? / ISO regulations?
Garantie? (...) / Guarantee? (...)

2. Organisatorische Anforderungen / Organizational requirements

2.1. Zeit-/Terminplan / Schedule
Entwicklungszeit? / Development time?
Inbetriebnahmezeit? / Startup time?
Reparaturzeit? (...) / Repair time? (...)

2.2. Personal / Staff
Kapazität, Qualifikation? / Capacity, qualification?
Werbung? / Advertising?
Kundendienst? / Customer service?
Lizenz- und Vertriebspartner? (...) / License and distribution partners? (...)

157

# MASCHINEN
### (für Maschinenbauer)

Maschinen.
Monumentale Maschinen,
metallene Montageschienen.
Motoren mit Millionen Millibar
mit mondänem Mantel, mit Minibar.
Mögliche Machbarkeit magnetisiert.
Motoren mäandern modellbasiert.
Maschinen.

Maschinen.
Monteure montieren Maschinen
manchmal mit manischen Mienen.
Maschinenbauers markantes Mandat:
multiple Modellbildung, Mikroformat
meldet Materialnutzungsgrade,
macht manchen Mann mächtig malade.
Maschinen.

Maschinen.
Modernste, mondänste Maschinen,
meist mit Mikrochip-Magazinen.
Menschliche Massenpsychose:
Maschinenmacht. Metamorphose.
Manchmal meucheln Malheure Maschinen
mit mahnenden Messeterminen.
Maschinen.

b. w.

# MACHINES

(for mechanical engineers)


Machines,
megalomanic machines.
Mechanic mastermind's masterstrokes modernize
mettlesome microchips, manoeuvres mesmerize,
microchips monitor momentous millibars,
marvelous motors, magnanimous minibars.
Mostly mepistophelean.
Machines.

Machines,
materialistic men's means:
machines make more money, make mothballs,
make marmalade,
mouthpieces, missiles, make marzipan, marinade,
money, more money, meticulous mastery.
Manic mechanics move motors majestically,
move measureless magazines.
Machines.

Machines,
minelayer's mighty machines.
Mechanist's main mandate: maximize, modulate,
microwaves misbehave, machine made masquerade.
Machinery masses, murderous mastermind,
machine mass morasses, menacing men, mankind.
Mindlessly misguided means.
Merrily mating machines.

pto

Maschinen – Maschinen
massakrieren Maschinen.
Menschenmordende Minen.
Manch Menschenfeind, mancher Magnat, Milliardär
maximiert Mordmacht, motorisiert Militär,
manche Mörderhand munitionierend,
Marodeurenmacht mobilisierend,
Maschinen.

Machines,
munitionizing machines.
Metamorphosis, mechanical millipedes,
mechanic mastermind modifies motors, meets
merchants, meets magnates, manipulates mightiness.
Makes machines murderous, marvelous, merciless.
Missiles meet mujahedeens.
Machines.

previously published in „Current Accounts", Bank Street Writers, Bolton/
UK, 2014; „The Transnational. A Literary Magazine", Vol. 2, UK, 2014

## TANZE MIT RAKETENSCHUHEN

(für Maschinenbauer)


Der Weltkulissenschieber stapelt die Patente tiefer,
die Kunst der Zentrifuge, unter Hochdruck der Ideen,
bringt Zeitzahnräder unter in dem schiefen Zahnradkiefer,
wo sie trotz der Reibung Kraft sich leise surrend drehen.
Er beschleunigt nun das Drehmoment in vierzehn
Arbeitsschritten,
das Mozartkugellager und die Baumkuchenmaschine,
im Anzug, schneidgebrannt und dazu
wasserstrahlgeschnitten,
und nimmt die Walze und die Kolben gegen die Routine.
Das magnetische Moment wird seine Dienste tun,
nicht ruhen,
das ist ein Rechnen, Reifen, Feilen, Schaffen, Schieben,
Schöpfen,
geh, feier' den Erfolg und tanze mit Raketenschuhen,
tanze himmelweit im Bogen über ihren Köpfen.


Hier noch ein Kopf, in dem die Räder ineinander greifen,
hier steht die Mutter aller Schrauben hoch im Kurs,
im Regelkreis,
wird jeden Schlagbaum unsichtbarer Grenzen einfach
schleifen,
zu viele Räder drehen sich bereits allein auf ihr Geheiß.
Verstummt sind Schall-Emissionäre, Kolbenfresserinnen,
das Bild verlässt allmählich seinen festgesteckten Rahmen.
Die Ansichten verändern sich nach außen wie nach innen,
Dynastien von Dynamos tragen künftig ihren Namen,

b. w.

## DANCE WITH ROCKET SHOES
(for mechanical engineers)


The world's scene-slider stacks the patents deeper
                till he sees
the art of the centrifuge under pressure of ideas
placing time cog wheels inside the slanting
                toothed-wheel jaw
where quietly rotating, they hum for the friction saw.
He accelerates the torque now in just fourteen
                working steps,
he takes the meat ball bearing and the drum machine
                perhaps,
in his suit that's water jet cut and fine flame burnt
                velveteen,
and he takes the rollers, plungers, hammers, nails
                against routine.
Magnetic moments do their service and they never rest,
this is a pushing, scooping, making, put it to the test.
Go! Celebrate the big success and dance with rocket shoes,
dance worlds apart, above their heads, across the avenues.


Here's a head within which all the wheels engage
                each other,
the female screw, of all the family members, it's
                the mother
who will grind down all the barriers to spread beyond
                the borders
,cause many wheels already turn according to her orders.
Sound emissionaries – silent cause she overcame
the noise, the image step by step will leave its settled
                frame.

pto

während Reichsbedenkenträger in den alten Truhen ruhen.
das ist ein Rechnen, Reifen, Feilen, Schaffen, Schieben,
Schöpfen,
geh, feier' den Erfolg und tanze mit Raketenschuhen,
tanze himmelweit im Bogen über ihren Köpfen.

Her name will once be carried by these dynasties of
            dynamos,
views will change, the range will change with every little
            mind she blows.
Put narrow minds in narrow cosy beds where they can rest.
This is a pushing, scooping, making, put it to the test.
Go! Celebrate the big success and dance with rocket shoes,
in an arc above their heads, across the avenues.

previously published in Bernadette Geyer (Editor): My Cruel Invention: A
Contemporary Poetry Anthology, Meerkat Press, 2015

# HERZSCHRITTMACHER
(für Elektrotechniker)

Sieh: Schienenbahnen für Trillionen zahme Elektronen,
die wir zu krönen planen auf Platinen-Großmissionen,
zack, zack, steck die Dose auf den Schockerstecker,
weck den letzten Schläfer mit Elektroschockerwecker,
bis bei Elektro-Techno frei die Funken sprühen,
vom Technik-Techtelmechtel alle Lampen glühen,
bis die Ovationen dröhnen, denn am Ende dienen
unsren Spleens die schönsten aller kühnen Maschinen.

Sieh: Steh'n im Tal und auf den Bergen hoch die Haare
im Wind durch wahre Wunderwerke,
                    Windkraft-Exemplare,
dann wird das alle faszinieren und elektrisieren
und in breiten Strömen sämig Strom für uns kreieren.
Wir bau'n mit Speed Metal im Kopf den Herzschrittmacher
und zum Elektro-Widerstand den Widersacher.
Der Morsecode der fein geplanten
                    Hochspannungskaskaden
lässt froher Nutzer Waden in Warmwasserschwaden baden.

## PACEMAKER

(for electrical engineers)


See: these plucky rail tracks, just crowned to eject tons
of billions, of ten trillions of tamed electrons,
chop, plug the jacks deeply into the sockets,
put stun gun alarm clocks in these sleeper's pockets,
electric entanglement lights up a spark,
techno electro plans glow in the dark.
The most daring of these tremendous machines
cause blooming ovations while lighting the scenes.

Wind works
wonders, wind lights up and down all the alleys,
see: hair standing up on the peaks, in the valleys,
electrifies, captivates us, so it seems,
creates electricity in creamy streams.
To build a real peacemaker, we'll build the pacemaker,
speed metal in our heads, seizing the heartbreaker.
Morse codes of these fine high-voltage cascades
let us wade in warm water for heady decades.

previously published in Bernadette Geyer (Editor): My Cruel Invention: A
Contemporary Poetry Anthology, Meerkat Press, 2015

## PFUSCH AM BAU

(für Bauingenieure)

Dafür war'n sie sich zu fein, die Pinkel.
Kein Wunder, dass da nichts mehr steht.
Da prüft man vorher mal die Winkel.
Die Träger waren nicht von Qualität.
Fast prähistorisch. Dann Gewimmer,
dass das auf Missverständnissen beruht.
Bauingenieure übrigens, noch immer,
verstehen sich stets ausgesprochen gut.
Korrupte Firmen, fachliche Verirrung,
Entscheidungswege überfrachtet.
Die ganze sprachliche Verwirrung
war gar nicht nötig, so betrachtet.
Das Unglück hat sich früh schon angebahnt.
Die ganze Statik war nicht recht durchdacht.
Der Turm von Babel war nicht gut geplant.
Schon der Vorentwurf – echt schlecht gemacht.

## BOTCHED BUILDING
(for civil engineers)


They were too stuck-up, all these prigs.
Such things collapse, it's a banality.
You have to check the angles, tools and jigs.
The drivers clearly had no quality.
Almost prehistoric. Dated skills.
„Misunderstandings", they complain.
Civil engineers communicate well, still.
Corrupt companies, professionals insane.
Decision paths completely overloaded.
The entire linguistic mess –
unnecessary till the thing imploded,
preventing a remarkable success.
Preliminary drafts were just a hurly burly.
No structural analyses, no doubt.
The disaster initiated early.
The Tower of Babel wasn't quite thought out.

**[GEDICHTTITEL HIER EINSETZEN]**
(für Informatiker)


[Untertitel des Gedichts durch Klicken hinzufügen]
Textfeld

Diese Zeile kann Änderungen an Ihrem Gedicht
hervorrufen
Wollen Sie diese Zeile behalten?
Behalten / Verwerfen
Es sind Updates verfügbar
Vertrauen Sie der Quelle?
Authentifiziert von „..."
Dieser Vorgang kann mehrere Minuten dauern
Fahren Sie das Gedicht nicht herunter
If your computer is infected with malware it may cause
your download to fail.

Update 1 von 7
Update 2 von 7
Update 3 von 7
Update 4 von 7
Update 5 von 7
Update 6 von 7
Update 7 von 7
Die Aktualisierung erfordert einen Neustart.
Wollen Sie das Gedicht jetzt neu starten?
Jetzt / später

Willkommen

Authentifizierung von „..." fehlgeschlagen
Virenreport 1 Trojaner
Status: gelöscht

## [INSERT TITLE OF THE POEM HERE]
(for computer scientists)


[Click to add subtitle of the poem]
Text box

Updates available
Do you trust the source?
Authentificated by „-"
This line may cause changes in your poem
Do you want to keep this line?
Keep / Discard
This may take a few minutes
Do not shutdown your poem
If your computer is infected with malware it may cause
your download to fail.


Update 1 of 7
Update 2 of 7
Update 3 of 7
Update 4 of 7
Update 5 of 7
Update 6 of 7
Update 7 of 7
The updates require a restart to take effect.
Do you want to restart the poem now?
Now / later


Welcome


Authentification of „-" failed
Virus report: 1 Trojan
Status = deleted

previously published in: Orbis #171, Spring 2015

## PROGRAMMIERER AN ASSISTENT
(für Informatiker)


Ich muss hier unbestritten
um jeden Button bitten,
wie plemplem auf allen Vieren
alles selbst implementieren.
Wenn Du blindlings
noch den Link links
mit dem Leistendings verlinkst,
lenkt das den Link links
auf die Stinklinks
von dem Scheißdings.
Wie Du anstrengst!
Ach, es langt längst.

(Statuszeile: gefeuert)

## PROGRAMMER TO ASSISTANT
(for computer scientists)


I still have to ask for everything,
you link the link
with this stinky thing
and let me implement
ev'ry complement.
No one hankers
for your flunking, shrinking links,
your rinky-dink honky-tonk bunkum stinks.
Shut down your button clutter,
I don't care what you mutter-stutter.
Cut off the bluff!
You fluffed enough.

(status line: fired)

## LAUTPOETISCHES PROTOKOLL DER REINI-
## GUNG EINER COMPUTERTASTATUR MIT UN-
## TERSCHIEDLICH VERSCHMUTZTEN TASTEN
## BEI EINGESCHALTETEM COMPUTER
### (für Informatiker)

hhgfgggggggggggggggggggggggggggggggggg
jjjjjjjjjjjhjhzhnghnhnnngbvuuuuuuuuuuuuuu
jujjjiiiiiiiiiiiiiiiiiiiiiiiiiiiiiiiiiiiiiiiiiiiiiiiiiiiiiiiiiikk
iiiiiiikkkk3errr3eeeeeeeeeeeeeeeeeeeerere
4wqqwsadsfdtzaaasSsnbbnnnnnnn
nnnnnnnnnnnnnnnnzzzzzzzzzz7ubvvvvvvvvvvvv
bbbbbgvfgvbbbvvbbbbbbbgiiiiiiiiiiiiiiiiiiiiiiiiiiii
iiiiooooiploloööölöööööökkkkkkkkkklll.ö----
Tztzztzzzzzztewsaaysaydaqssaqysyyyyy,,,,,,,,,,,,,,,,,,,
9oioiokk,iukccfvviiiiiiiiiiiiiiiiiiiiiiiiiiiiiiiiiiiooiopü
Äöä-.l--.,m. m,mnbvbnm,mxcx...aysxdcfgvbhjnmk,l.ö-ä
AAAAAAAAAAAAAAAAAAAAAAAAAq
1weerwqerwrwrtzui.-.10232222222222211111
nnnnnh 0ß900ßß90iokl09iopkl-+., üßü++

(Bemerkung des Autors: gekürzt, Absätze, Leerzeichen sowie semantopho-
netisch wenig autarke Zeichen wurden aus Gründen der Druckkostenerspar-
nis weitgehend entfernt)

174

## SOUND POETIC MINUTES OF THE CLEANING OF A COMPUTER KEYBOARD WITH DIFFERENTLY DIRTY KEYS WHILE THE COMPUTER IS TURNED ON

(for computer scientists)


hgfgggggggggggggggggggggggggggggggggg
jjjjjjjjjjjhjhzhnghnhnnngbvuuuuuuuuuuuuuu
jujjjiiiiiiiiiiiiiiiiiiiiiiiiiiiiiiiiiiiiiiiiiiiiiiiiiiiiiiiiiiiiikk
iiiiiiikkkk3errr3eeeeeeeeeeeeeeeeeeeeerere
4wqqwsadsfdtzaaasSsntbnnnnnnn
nnnnnnnnnnnnnnnnzzzzzzzzzzz7ubvvvvvvvvvvvv
bbbbbgvfgvbbbvvbbbbbbbgiiiiiiiiiiiiiiiiiiiiiiiiiiiii
iiiiooooiploloööölöööööö3kkkkkkkkkkklll.ö----
Tztzztzzzzzzztewsaaysaydaqssaqysyyyyy,,,,,,,,,,,,,,,,,,,,
9oioiokk,iukccfvviiiiiiiiiiiiiiiiiiiiiiiiiiiiiiiiiiiiiiooiopü
Āöä-.l--.,m. m,mnbvbnm,mxcx...aysxdcfgvbhjnmk,l.ö-ä
AAAAAAAAAAAAAAAAAAAAAAAAq
1weerwqerwrwrtzui.-.10232222222222211111
nnnnnh  0ß900ßß90iokl09iopkl-+., üßü++


(Editorial note 1: read aloud.

Editorial note 2: paragraphs, empty spaces and semantically non-autarkic characters were largely removed to reduce printing costs.)

**BONUS**

Foto Ellen Eckhardt

**DUMMHEIT UND APPLAUS**
(für Medienwissenschaftler)

Es steht Spitz auf Knopf und Kopf, so wie es steht.
Jetzt beginnt die große Abendschau.
Zunächst wurde die Wirklichkeit TV
und dann wieder TV Realität.
Belohnt man Dummheit mit Applaus,
bis sie die Welt beherrscht, dann sieh:
alles wird Reality TV,
es walzt dich platt und schaltet dich dann aus.
Wer braucht denn Anstand und Talent,
wer Wissen, Umsicht oder Rücksicht,
ungebremst sieht man so schön dein Rücklicht,
ohne all das wirst du Präsident.

10/11/2016

**BONUS**


## THE VOW OF AHMED EL SHALOW
(for theologians)


The giant Ahmed el Shalhow
praised the Gods and filed a vow
to shit a sketch of mighty Brahma
in thirty years, helped by his llamas,
with runs and normal bowel movement
to achieve karma improvement
into the steppe country side,
from edge to edge, just two miles wide,
admired from a mesa's top.
The people came and wouldn't stop
to praise the way it was arranged,
but suddenly the climate changed,
the growing desert was it's fate:
a drifting sand dune, seen too late,
now getting closer day by day,
just polished Ahmed's sketch away,
stopped celebrating enthusiasts.
In this life, nothing ever lasts.
It ruined Ahmed's God portrait.
„Now, holy shit", some heard him say.


previously published in: Jonathan MS Pearce (Editor): Filling The Void: A
Selection Of Humanist And Atheist Poetry, Onus Books, 2016
Deutsches Pendant in „Glasaugenstern", chiliverlag, 2015

**wir wölfe** – Gedichte
Eine poetische Hommage an unsere Tierwelt
Anthologie, Hrsg. Franziska Röchter
Mit Fotos von Heike Großmann und Christine Zeides
chiliverlag, Juli 2016, ISBN 978-3-943292-45-9
148 Seiten, Euro 9,90

Annähernd 60 Autorinnen und Autoren, unter ihnen Michael Starcke, Peter Ettl, Esther Ackermann, Thomas Rackwitz, Sören Heim, dichten über die Vielfalt und den Artenreichtum unserer Tierwelt. Aus den Gedichten und den Fotos von Heike Großmann und Christine Zeides spricht eine große Wertschätzung gegenüber Tieren und ein Erkennen ihrer unglaublichen Einzigartigkeit sowie Bewunderung ihrer Schönheit.

Mal humorvoll, zunehmend aber auch ernsthaft werden Besonderheiten einiger Tierarten und Wissenswertes poetisch beleuchtet und ihr Dasein in Relation zum Menschen bespiegelt. Mit Gedichten des Anfang 2016 verstorbenen Bochumer Lyrikers Michael Starcke.

**Pappalappa Mirzapan** – Gedichte für besondere Kinder
Anthologie, Hrsg. Franziska Röchter
Mit einem Nachwort von Bernhard Winter
chiliverlag, November 2016, ISBN 978-3-943292-49-7
80 Seiten, 8,90 Euro

Rund 35 Autorinnen und Autoren, unter ihnen Alex Dreppec, Bernhard Winter, Jürgen Völkert-Marten, Elisabeth Drab u. v. m. schreiben Gedichte für ganz besondere Kinder.

Dieses ganz besondere Büchlein gibt Eltern Gedichte an die Hand, um ein Sprachverständnis selbst bei denjenigen Kindern und Jugendlichen zu fördern, von denen man annimmt, sie hätten nicht die nötigen Voraussetzungen, um Gedichte zu verstehen. Ein wunderbarer Band zur spielerischen Unterstützung von Sprachanbahnung und -entwicklung bei Spezialkindern, aber ebenso bei allen anderen Kindern, die Klang, Rhythmus und Stimme genießen und an Versen und Reimen Spaß haben. Mit einem Nachwort von Bernhard Winter, psychologischer Psychotherapeut und Lyriker.

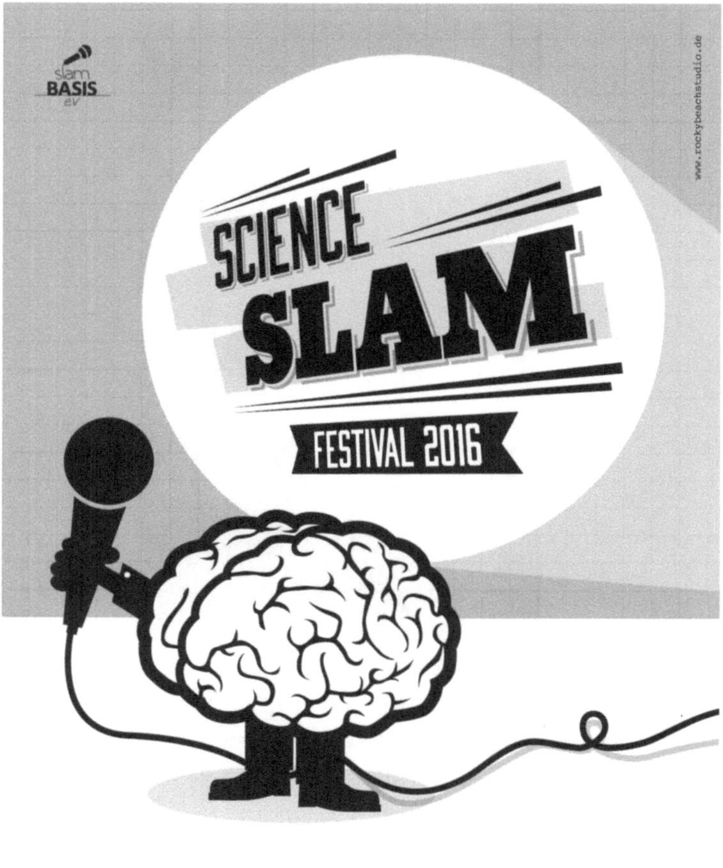

# 10 JAHRE SCIENCE SLAM

## Science-Slam-Best-of-Show
16.12.2016, 19:30 Uhr
Centralstation

## 7. Deutsche Science-Slam-Meisterschaft
17.12.2016, 20:00 Uhr
Darmstadtium

Weitere Termine und Infos unter www.scienceslam2016.de
Tickets unter www.ztix.de